BROKE MILLENNIAL

"[*Broke Millennial*] is well written and researched by a millennial for millennials. You hear their voices and their concerns without the judgment, sarcasm, and superiority we older folks too often convey when we talk to young adults about money."   —*The Washington Post*

"A new book about money that teens and millennials will actually read . . . This not only has great insights and tips about handling money . . . it's written in a casual, relatable way."
                                                                                                    —*Time*

"If you haven't quite got the hang of 'adulting,' follow Erin Lowry's spot-on, often funny financial advice."
           —Lynnette Khalfani-Cox, cofounder of AskTheMoneyCoach.com and *New York Times* bestselling author of *Zero Debt: The Ultimate Guide to Financial Freedom*

"*Broke Millennial* takes the typical preaching out of money lessons and replaces it with humor, empathy, and a fun, pick-your-financial-path twist, for successfully navigating all the financial questions you'll face in the real world."
           —Farnoosh Torabi, financial expert and host of the award-winning podcast *So Money*

"This is the ultimate millennial guidebook on personal finance. Erin Lowry does a great job of reducing jargon and sharing knowledge that is practical and actionable. If there is a book you must read to get your financial life together, I highly recommend *Broke Millennial*."
           —Jason Vitug, bestselling author of *You Only Live Once: The Roadmap to Financial Wellness and a Purposeful Life*

BROKE MILLENNIAL TAKES ON INVESTING

"By the time you're done reading, you'll know exactly how to buy and sell and stock, why investing earlier rather than later is a good idea, and how to get started on the road to wealth. If you're insecure about investing and need some beginner help, this book may be exactly what you need."

—*Forbes*

"Erin Lowry delivers simple, easy-to-digest advice on how to tackle tricky money problems in the modern age. Should you invest while paying down student loans? How do you talk to your partner about money? Are robo-advisors and investing apps actually helpful? Stop wondering and start getting your financial life together."

—CNBC Make It

"Erin makes even the most difficult-to-understand financial concepts into something you actually want to talk about. If you are intimidated (or, frankly, bored) by the idea of investing, let Erin prove you wrong on both counts with this fantastic book."

—Chelsea Fagan, cofounder of TheFinancialDiet.com and coauthor of *The Financial Diet*

BROKE MILLENNIAL TALKS MONEY

"This is Erin Lowry's best book yet. After reading *Broke Millennial Talks Money*, you'll no longer shy away from money discussions with your coworkers, friends, family members, or romantic partners. You'll be ready to talk!"

—Cameron Huddleston, author of *Mom and Dad, We Need to Talk: How to Have Essential Conversations with Your Parents About Their Finances*

"Learning how to talk about money is the first step in making more of it. While the focus may be on money, this book is really about the relationships we have with one another and what we value in our lives. It is straightforward, engaging, and relatable. I highly recommend it for everyone—not just millennials!"

—Claire Wasserman, founder and author of *Ladies Get Paid*

"Money conversations aren't the sexiest tactic in personal finance, but they're fundamental to reaching your financial goals. If you've been stalling, this book takes 'I don't know where to start' off the table!"

—Kiersten Saunders, cofounder of Rich & Regular and coauthor of *Cashing Out*

BROKE
MILLENNIAL
Workbook

BROKE MILLENNIAL WORKBOOK

Take Control and Get Your Financial Life Together

Erin Lowry

A TarcherPerigee Book

tarcherperigee

an imprint of Penguin Random House LLC
penguinrandomhouse.com

Most TarcherPerigee books are available at special quantity discounts for bulk purchase for sales promotions, premiums, fund-raising, and educational needs. Special books or book excerpts also can be created to fit specific needs. For details, write: SpecialMarkets@penguinrandomhouse.com.

Trade paperback ISBN: 9780593541357

Printed in the United States of America
1st Printing

This is for every broke millennial (or Gen Xer or Boomer or Gen Zer)
who has struggled with financial anxiety and fear

Contents

Chapter 1

An Introduction: Money Isn't the Worst! Seriously.

HELLO THERE!

Welcome to *Broke Millennial Workbook,* a resource to help you take actionable steps to get your financial life together.

I'm Erin Lowry, your guide/narrator/financial translator to help you along the journey.

I've written about money for more than a decade and consulted both friends and complete strangers about basic personal finance topics. Unfortunately, it's clear to me that even with a massive influx in access to personal finance information and education, so much anxiety about money still exists. This needs to be fixed *now.* Failure to do so means setting yourself up for a life of mental and emotional stress. That may sound dramatic, but no one deserves to live in the anxiety of a paycheck-to-paycheck cycle or fretting about the smallest unexpected expense upending their entire lives.

The good news is that you can break free of that (or avoid it entirely), and I'll show you how. Despite what Wall Street and some media outlets want you to believe, money isn't complicated, and it doesn't require the mastery of complex formulas. Financial empowerment does, however, require taking actionable steps toward improving your situation, and I'm here to help you figure out those steps.

I started *Broke Millennial* back in January of 2013 as a hobby and then a side hustle. It was a blog back in those days, but has since developed into a three-part book series and my full-time job. My work has helped hundreds of thousands of people reframe their relationship with money and take back control.

HOLD UP—DO I HAVE TO BUY ANOTHER BOOK TO DO THIS?

No, you absolutely don't.

This workbook is largely based on *Broke Millennial: Stop Scraping By and Get Your Financial Life Together*, but includes a smattering of insights from *Broke Millennial Takes On Investing* and *Broke Millennial Talks Money*.

It stands completely on its own, and you won't be asked to refer to any of the other books in the series in order to complete exercises. Sure, you might find it helpful to read those as well to continue on your financial journey, but you can do this workbook with no prior reading of the Broke Millennial series!

I HATE BORING FINANCIAL STUFF, SO WHY SHOULDN'T I PUT THIS BOOK DOWN RIGHT NOW?

First of all, this workbook isn't a boring lecture on money. (The world doesn't need another one of those.) It's developed around the reality that personal finance is *personal*, so you should be able to create a strategy and a system that work best for you personally. Whether you complete it chronologically or flip through at random, each chapter will give you actionable exercises and advice on how to improve and further strengthen your relationship with money.

The first few chapters lay the foundation for your journey toward building a healthy financial life. Exercises in these chapters will help you discover your personal relationship with money and what psychological blocks or pitfalls may surround it for you, as well as show you how to assess your financial know-how and improve it.

Then we'll tackle a host of topics ranging from budgeting to credit cards, paying down debt, and managing student loans. Many of the chapters address sticky situations millennials specifically face, such as negotiating your salary, navigating those awkward times when friendships and finances collide (like what to do when you can't afford to split the dinner bill evenly with your pals), and getting financially naked with your partner. You'll even learn a bit about investing, which, spoiler alert, isn't just for wealthy people!

There will be some financial jargon used—hard to avoid in a finance book—but it's mostly a safe space for you to learn about money with more than a dash of humor. By the end, you're going to feel confident instead of terrorized each time you balance your budget. Like I said, managing your money can be enjoyable . . . and even, dare I say, fun.

HOW TO INTERACT WITH THIS WORKBOOK

Basically however you want! You should start with chapters 2 and 3 to lay some important foundational work, which will be referenced in other chapters. But once you're done with those, you can jump to whichever chapters are relevant or simply most appealing. Well, it might be most helpful if you start with the chapters that sound the least appealing (I'm guessing budgets and student loans). But hey, this is your financial journey and *you* get to decide!

Okay, let's *get your financial life together.* #GYFLT.

Chapter 2

Is Money a Tinder Date or Marriage Material?

GUESS WHAT?! The first step in getting a grasp on your financial situation doesn't involve any math (yay!). In fact, managing money isn't complicated at all and doesn't involve complex formulas. One of the most common but infuriating excuses I hear is: "I'm not good at math, so I'm not good with money."

Instead of spiraling about math, you need to be thinking about psychology. A critical part of taking control of your financial life is understanding your relationship with money.

The way you handle money is primarily driven by your mental attitude toward it. This attitude started developing in your childhood and was reinforced by the people who raised you and the people you were around. What you saw and experienced as a kid has a direct impact on how you handle your money today.

You might already be sensing that even though this section requires zero math and offers up no formulas, it's not easy. Do not skip it!

The exercises in this chapter create the foundation for your financial journey (and the rest of this workbook). Skipping it is like trying to put together Ikea or Wayfair furniture without the instructions, and we all know it feels mind-boggling even *with* the instructions! You need to decide if you treat your finances as a hit-it-and-forget-it situation or if you're developing a long-lasting relationship. Basically, is money a Tinder date or marriage material? (Not to disparage people who have found everlasting love on Tinder! But let's be honest: You're the exception and not the rule.)

EXERCISE
FEEL YOUR FEELS

Take a moment to think about money. I know that sounds a little strange, but just think "money." How does just that word make you feel? Go on, write down a few words to describe how you're feeling right now.

_____.

_____.

_____.

These feelings provide insight into your relationship with money. We all have an emotional relationship with money. It's that relationship dynamic that impacts a lot about how we handle our finances. Maybe you feel so good about saving that you tip into a money-hoarding, doomsday-prepping mentality. Or perhaps you feel so good about spending that you just avoid checking your bank accounts or credit cards because you know the situation looks bleak.

Take a moment to reflect on what you tend to do with "surprise" money. For example, you get a bonus at work or your tax refund hits your bank account or your parents send you some cash as a birthday present. Where does that money usually end up?

$50 in surprise money would be _____.

$100 in surprise money would be _____.

$500 in surprise money would be _____.

$1,000 in surprise money would be _____.

ARE YOU BEING HONEST?

Were you honest with yourself or are you being the idealized version of yourself?

It's okay if it was the latter. We all have moments of fixating on our idealized selves. I've definitely purchased overpriced leggings, thinking that I'd be more likely to end up on my yoga mat if I "invested" in the expensive workout gear, or that I'd finally learn a new skill if I just splurged on an educational course. Usually, that's not how it works. I end up on my yoga mat in my ratty old sweatpants because I've prioritized doing yoga today, not because I bought expensive leggings.

But for the sake of these exercises, and moving forward with getting your financial life together, you need to be brutally honest with yourself. It might feel painful to admit certain truths and to physically write them down. That's okay. The only way to move forward and actually take control of your finances is to be honest with yourself, especially about psychological blocks you have around money.

On the off chance you weren't radically honest with yourself about what you'd do with surprise money, here's another chance to answer the questions:

$50 in surprise money would be _____.

$100 in surprise money would be _____.

$500 in surprise money would be _____.

$1,000 in surprise money would be _____.

I'll share my truth with you: I have an intense scarcity mindset around money. That means I have a persistent, nagging worry that I'll lose my financial stability.

It's a mindset that on paper makes no sense. Scarcity mindset is often attributed to growing up in a financially unstable situation or having a tough time as an adult. My childhood was financially stable, and while I went through times of making very little money as a young adult, I was always able to pay my bills and cover my basic needs.

This mindset also frustrates me because, on paper, I shouldn't have this anxiety. I haven't experienced a total job loss and in fact have multiple streams of income. Even during slow seasons within my profession, I've never been entirely without income. I have a healthy emergency savings fund. I have the proper health, life, renters, and auto insurances to be prepared for the unexpected. I even have a prenup, which I consider marriage insurance. Despite all the evidence, the scarcity mentality persists.

I share this with you because it's okay if you work through this section and discover you have some tough psychological blocks. You might even be surprised about what you uncover. Unfortunately, you probably aren't going to heal your mindset quickly. In fact, it might be so ingrained that you never permanently shake it off. Instead, you learn how to work with or around your blocks.

EXERCISE
TAKING INVENTORY OF YOUR FINANCIAL ROADBLOCKS

If you've never considered your financial mindset before, that's completely normal. Money is often taught both in mathematical terms and with the belief that willpower and gumption are all you need to take control. Well, surprise, that's not the full picture. Your emotions are possibly the most powerful force when it comes to how you handle money. Identifying why you feel the way you do about money requires a little bit of exploration into your past.

These questions should help you start to identify triggers you might have around money—such as compulsions to spend or why you're fixated on saving or why you believe frugality is of the utmost importance.

Pick up your favorite pen and start answering the questions below. It's okay if you need to step away or come back after a break. These questions could start to stir up some strong emotions and memories.

What's your first memory of money? How does that memory make you feel?

_____.

_____.

_____.

_____.

_____.

_____.

_____.

_____.

How did you get money to spend growing up?

_____.

_____.

_____.

_____.

When you had money to spend in your childhood, what did you buy?

_____.

_____.

_____.

_____.

When you have money to spend today, what's the first thing you want to buy?

_____.

_____.

_____.

_____.

What are your financial concerns today?

_____.

_____.

_____.

_____.

Why do you have these concerns?

_____.

_____.

_____.

_____.

How did your parents talk about money when you were a kid?

_____.

_____.

_____.

_____.

Were you told that asking about money was rude or inappropriate?

_____.

_____.

_____.

Did your family's financial situation make you uncomfortable around your peers?

_____.

_____.

_____.

_____.

Are you taking actionable steps to ensure that your fears don't happen (e.g., saving to make sure you can always pay rent or your mortgage even if you lose your job)?

_____ .

_____ .

_____ .

_____ .

ARE YOU NOTICING PATTERNS OF SELF-SABOTAGE?

You've done some of the initial heavy lifting to unpack your emotional relationship with money, but it could leave you with this nagging sensation that you tend to self-sabotage your finances. Don't be too self-critical; that's really common behavior. The hard part can be decoding the why.

You may need guidance figuring out why—despite having all the information about how to handle money—you keep self-sabotaging.

A friend of mine—let's call her Leslie—is well versed in how to budget, save, and invest. She knows all the information. She goes through periods of creating financial stability for herself by saving and spending within her means. But for some reason, Leslie consistently goes through periods of compulsive spending, which result in her having to use her savings to pay off credit card bills and bringing her right back into a precarious financial situation. Leslie eventually began to realize that she grew up in a financially chaotic environment and that even though it's stressful, financial chaos is her comfort zone. It's what she knows and understands. Her inclination is to self-sabotage to take her back to a financial situation she grew up around.

There are a multitude of reasons people seek out therapy, but did you know there is such a thing as financial therapy? It exists because you sometimes need help untangling all of your complicated feelings around money and learning how to rebuild.

For financial therapist Lindsay Bryan-Podvin, *having a balanced relationship with money is being able to view money as a neutral or a positive, meaning it doesn't cause angst and it isn't the foundation of your happiness either.*

Financial therapy will help you unpack your cognitive and emotional relationships to money, which may stand in your way of having a healthy relationship to money.

Dr. Brad Klontz, a financial therapist and professor of financial psychology at Creighton University, describes money disorders as "chronic patterns of self-destructive financial behavior. We know better, but we just can't seem to stop ourselves."

EXERCISE
REASONS TO CONSIDER FINANCIAL THERAPY

Let's be honest: We probably all have a self-destructive financial behavior or two. Do you think you can identify yours? Take a moment to reflect and write down some of your financial behaviors that you'd like to stop or improve.

Here are behaviors with money I want to stop or improve:

_____.

_____.

_____.

_____.

Not everyone will need to seek counsel from a financial therapist in order to improve their destructive financial behaviors. However, if you find yourself in a consistent cycle of financial self-sabotage, it might be worth exploring.

Here are some behaviors to consider. Check the boxes that apply to you.

❏ You'd consider yourself a workaholic.

❏ You overshare details about your financial issues (or the family's) with your children.

❏ You feel compelled to shop or buy a treat when you're experiencing an intense emotion.

❏ You keep making purchases of nonessential goods, even though you know you can't afford them.

❏ You consistently gamble money you can't afford to lose.

❏ You use money as a way to control relationship dynamics in your life.

❏ Money is being used as a tool to control you by someone in your life (e.g., being withheld if you don't behave in a certain way).

❏ You are hiding money behaviors (spending, investing, saving) from a partner.

❏ You're extremely frugal and find it hard to spend money, even if you need to.

Want to learn more about your own money scripts and disorders?

Take the Klontz Money Script Inventory at https://www.bradklontz.com/moneyscripts test.

As of 2022, financial therapy is still a fairly new field, so Klontz advises that you seek out a licensed mental health provider as your financial therapist. You can refer to the Financial Therapy Association's website in order to search for a financial therapist.

An Important Consideration: Your financial therapist should not be the person who is managing your money, even if he or she is also a certified financial planner or financial advisor of any sort.

TIME AND MONEY
But Probably Not in the Way You're Thinking!

Have you ever considered the way in which you relate to time? I don't mean what time it is right now. I mean the past, present, and future. Do you fixate on mulling over things that happened in the past or really stay present—so much so that you never consider the future consequences of your behaviors? Or maybe you just love daydreaming and planning for your future?

A fintech company I once worked for conducted a study[1] based on Dr. Philip Zimbardo and Dr. John Boyd's work, *The Time Paradox*. The study focused on how people's relationship to time directly impacts their financial health. Our fixations on the past, present, or future can inform how we spend or save. It might sound a bit quirky, but it will become more clear as you work through this exercise.

Inspired by this work, I've come up with a few common "money teams" people tend to gravitate toward and how they impact our wallets.

EXERCISE
WHICH MONEY TEAM HAVE YOU JOINED?

Ready to find out which team you play for? Check four statements below that most sound like something you'd say (or have said).

- ❏ "Drinks are on me." [**1 point**]

- ❏ "I'll worry about putting money into my 401(k) when I pay off my student loans." [**2 points**]

- ❏ "Sorry, I'm going to pick up this extra shift instead of coming out tonight." [**3 points**]

- ❏ "Shit, I just went overdraft again. No worries, I can charge it on my credit card." [**1 point**]

- ❏ "I don't believe in investing for retirement. I'll just make a lot of money instead." [**2 points**]

❏ "I should probably increase my 401(k) contribution." [**3 points**]

❏ "I was going to quit that job anyway." [**1 point**]

❏ "I'll for sure be making twice my current salary in the next five years." [**2 points**]

❏ "Side hustles are pretty awesome. I've saved a ton of extra money." [**3 points**]

❏ "I'd like to save more, but I'll worry about that when I make more." [**2 points**]

❏ "It sounds like a fun trip, but I'm really focused on saving up for a down payment." [**3 points**]

❏ "Budgets just get in the way of living life." [**1 point**]

Total points _____

Decoding Your Score

A score between 4 to 6 points means . . .

You're TEAM YOLOFOMO. Your social media accounts might look #blessed, #killinit, and #livingthedream—but your finances are probably more #brokemillennial. Yes, experiences are valuable, but the lifestyle choice of focusing on the present and allowing "YOLO" and "FOMO" to heavily influence your decisions could mean you're #WorkingUntilYouDie.

A score between 7 to 9 points means . . .

You're TEAM GUARDED OPTIMIST. Do you have a potentially delusional vision of where you and your salary will be in the next five to ten years? It's okay. We all secretly do to some degree. But to avoid any nasty surprises down the road, it's important to work on being proactive about the reality of your finances today and start to lay groundwork for a financially stable future, just in case your idealized vision of the future never quite materializes in the way you planned.

A score between 10 to 12 points . . .

You're TEAM DREAMING ABOUT RETIREMENT. Being hyper-focused on the future is financially beneficial in that it can lead to a well-funded 401(k), hefty emergency savings, and probably some additional investments. However, it's not all puppy cuddles and blue skies. Pulling a Scrooge McDuck in order to have piles of money in the future could come at the cost of sacrificing relationships and only having memories of long nights at work because you failed to live a little in the present.

This is a kitschy way to engage your brain in figuring out a little bit of how you relate to money, but all of these teams do actually have merit. A healthy balance of all three teams is where we should all strive to be. It's okay to splurge, make memories, and live it up sometimes. You should be optimistic about your abilities and what you can achieve. But you also want to be proactive and build the foundation for your future by putting in the work today. It might feel damn near impossible to have a consistent balance of all three teams at any given time, but that doesn't mean we should stop trying.

EXERCISE
GOAL SETTING

Now that you've spent time considering your emotional relationship to money, it's time to write three financial goals to help improve (or heal) this dynamic.

In the next 30 days, I will:

_____.

_____.

_____.

_____.

In the next six months, I will:

_____.

_____.

_____.

_____.

In the next year, I will:

_____.

_____.

_____.

_____.

Feeling stuck? That's okay! This is all a lot to process. Here are a few ideas to get your thinking juices flowing.

For the next month, take ten minutes every day to do at least one exercise in this workbook or read a few pages.

Do you want to get over a fear of investing? Set a goal to research and understand basic investing terminology in the next six months and have $1,000 set aside to put into the stock market.

Perhaps a longer-term goal is to model a healthier relationship with money for your children (or nieces and nephews or friends' kids) than you had modeled to you.

UP NEXT

Now that you've started to identify some of your roadblocks and some of your potential hang-ups around money, let's talk about where you should probably head next. As you might remember from chapter 1, this workbook doesn't have to be completed cover to cover. In fact, I encourage you to jump around if that motivates you to keep working on getting your financial life together. Here are suggested next steps, depending on your money team.

TEAM YOLOFOMO

- Chapter 3: Do You Have a Gold Star in Personal Finance?

- Chapter 4: Dealing with the Dreaded B-Word

- Chapter 6: Credit Reports and Scores: The Report Card for Life

- Chapter 7: Wait, *This* Is How I'm Supposed to Use My Credit Cards?!

- Chapter 8: Yikes, I Have Debt. What Now?

- Chapter 10: Life Is Already Overwhelmingly Expensive. Do I Really Have to Focus on Saving?

TEAM GUARDED OPTIMIST

- Chapter 3: Do You Have a Gold Star in Personal Finance?

- Chapter 4: Dealing with the Dreaded B-Word

- Chapter 6: Credit Reports and Scores: The Report Card for Life

- Chapter 7: Wait, *This* Is How I'm Supposed to Use My Credit Cards?!

- Chapter 10: Life Is Already Overwhelmingly Expensive. Do I Really Have to Focus on Saving?

- Chapter 13: How to Negotiate Salary (or Anything Else) by Learning to Ask for What You Want

TEAM DREAMING ABOUT RETIREMENT

- -

GET YOUR FINANCIAL LIFE TOGETHER CHECK-IN

We're not entirely ready to move on quite yet. Instead, this is your first GYFLT check-in. I'll be asking you to do a quick reflection at the end of each chapter. You might be rolling your eyes a bit right now, but Future You is going to have a lot of fun rereading these answers and charting your progress toward taking control and getting your financial life together!

What is your biggest takeaway (or aha moment) from this chapter?

_____.

_____.

_____.

What feels the most overwhelming about this chapter?

_____.

_____.

_____.

Why does it feel so overwhelming to you in this moment?

_____.

_____.

_____.

Based on what you just learned, write down one actionable step you can take this week to improve your financial life.

_____.

_____.

_____.

Chapter 3

Do You Have a Gold Star in Personal Finance?

IN THE LAST CHAPTER, you started to address your potential roadblocks when it comes to money. Now we're going to bring in the math. It's time to get a better understanding of the pieces that make up your financial puzzle—and how to put that puzzle together. But first, I must confess something.

There is a singular frustrating truth when it comes to your personal finances. The answer to any money question is almost always "It depends." It depends because, as the saying goes, "Personal finance is *personal*." The exact strategies that work for me aren't necessarily what are going to work for you. What works for you might not be what works for your parent, partner, best friend, sibling, or coworkers. Now you know the dirty little secret of the personal finance and larger financial planning industry!

You might be thinking, "Wait, what?! You were going to tell me exactly how to take control of my financial life!"

Don't worry—I'll be giving you plenty of directions and actionable advice. However, it's important for you to know that there should always be nuance and shades of gray in financial discussions. But people often don't want nuance. We crave benchmarks and charts and ways for us to compare ourselves to how others are doing or where we "should" be at this stage in our lives.

So, even with that caveat, in this chapter you're going to learn many of the common benchmarks and even—*gasp*—formulas that are used in personal finance. These can be used to assess your current status in your financial journey and help you set goals for the future.

Keep in mind that these are simply standard rules of thumb. These rules don't know you or your goals or how far you've already come. Do not be demoralized if your current situation is below where the benchmark says you should be at your age. You're taking the actionable steps right now to build that strong financial future.

Let's start with a critical method to stabilize your financial life.

ASSESSING YOUR EMERGENCY FUND

An emergency fund is like creating your own insurance policy against disaster. (You should still have adequate insurance, though!) The aim of an emergency fund is to save money in an easily accessible way and not to touch it unless you face a legitimate emergency. And no, Beyoncé announcing a pop-up concert does not count as an emergency!

Did You Know: Prevailing personal finance advice is to have at least three to six months of basic living expenses saved in your emergency fund. However, the COVID-19 pandemic taught us all that even six months might not be enough. You need to consider your own risk tolerance and how much you need to feel comfortable—which will probably depend on the stability of your income. For the sake of this section, I will use the standard rule of thumb, but you are free to adjust.

Emergency Fund Formula

$$\frac{\text{Cash \& Cash Equivalents*}}{\text{Amount you need to cover your basic needs}} = \text{three to six months of living expenses}$$

For example: You need $3,500 a month to cover all your bare essential living expenses like housing, utilities, cell phone, debt payments, groceries, insurance, childcare, and transportation. You currently have $4,300 in a savings account.

---

* Cash equivalents refer to invested money that's easily accessible and converted into cash. For example, money market funds or certificates of deposits (CDs).

$$\frac{(\$4,300)}{(\$3,500)} = 1.23 \text{ months covered}$$

WHERE TO KEEP YOUR EMERGENCY FUND

Your emergency fund should be kept in a plain old savings account. You don't want to invest this money because you don't want it to be put at any risk. Murphy's Law probably means that your emergency, like a job loss, would coincide with the stock market not performing well. You don't want to have to sell your investments in a down market because you're desperate for cash and didn't leave any in savings.

But speaking of savings . . . how much interest are you earning on your savings account? You don't know? Go look it up right now!

Helpful Hint: Not sure how to look it up? Log in to your account and look for "account details." It will either be written as "interest rate" or "APY," which stands for "annual percentage yield." Or just Google the name of your bank and the type of savings account you have.

My savings account is earning _____% APY.

Did You Know: The APY on savings accounts fluctuates over time. In 2018, it was common to have at least 2.00% APY, but then rates started to drop again. In early 2022, it was common to have 0.50% APY—but that started to rise to 0.90% APY by the middle of the year and 2.00% APY by the fall of 2022. Just know that you can do better than a zero after the decimal point! If your rate is 0.01% or 0.05%, then it's time to move that savings to a place where it earns a little more money!

EXERCISE
YOUR SECONDARY EMERGENCY SAFETY NET

Your emergency fund safety net is much more than cash on hand. Six months of living expenses saved is an admirable goal. However, you should also consider your nonfinancial safety net. Let's assess other options you have in a worst-case scenario by thinking about your network, which can span from loved ones to acquaintances to community services.

Who in your network of friends, family, or coworkers could help you get a job (or job interview)?

_____.

_____.

Who could you temporarily move in with if you needed a place to stay?

_____.

_____.

Who could you turn to for a loan?

_____.

_____.

Who could help with childcare?

_____.

_____.

Who could help with transportation needs?

_____.

_____.

What services are available in your community that you could use in a personal financial crisis?

_____.

_____.

Helpful Hint: Unsure how to search for programs? Try FindHelp.org or feeding america.org/find-your-local-foodbank.

We're going to do some more emergency fund exercises in chapter 10. You can flip ahead if this is a critical area of concern for you!

FINANCIAL FORMULAS AND BENCHMARKS TO KNOW

People are judgmental. Let's just admit it. We scroll through social media and compare our lives to the carefully curated ones our friends and influencers have created for themselves. It is a natural instinct to make comparisons, so it makes sense that we would do it with our financial situations.

For some people, it can be beneficial to compare yourself to the savings, debt, and investing averages of your peers. It can be motivational and help you stay on track. For others, it can feel demoralizing. How do you feel?

I feel _____ *when I read about where I should be with my finances.*

If your answer was upset, sad, frustrated, demoralized, or something similar, then consider this your permission to opt out of the benchmark-specific exercises below. I highly encourage you to still work through the formula ones (like debt-to-income ratio and net worth). Having these numbers will be helpful later on in your process with this workbook.

Everyone, regardless of feelings toward benchmarks, should complete the final exercise in this chapter about setting your own benchmarks.

DEBT-TO-INCOME RATIO

Debt-to-income (DTI) ratio is exactly what it sounds like: You're calculating the percentage of debt you owe relative to the amount of money you're earning.

Lenders use DTI as a key element in lending decisions to calculate if you can handle more debt. The higher your debt-to-income ratio, the less likely you can afford another loan. A high DTI would be a percentage north of 36. Staying in the low twenties or below makes you much more competitive as a candidate for a loan. In the single digits? Those lenders are going to have the serious hots for you!

The calculation looks like this:

$$\frac{\text{(Monthly debt payments)}}{\text{(Gross monthly income)}} = \text{DTI}$$

EXERCISE
LET'S CALCULATE YOUR DTI

Understanding the Formula

- *Monthly debt payment* means the debt you've taken on like student loans, car loans, housing payments, or balances on credit cards that you're paying off in monthly installments. You aren't calculating the total amount of debt you owe, just those monthly payments toward the total. For example, you owe $10,000 in student loans and $5,000 in credit card debt. You pay $100 per month toward student loans and $150 per month toward your credit cards. Your monthly debt payment would be $250.

- *Gross monthly income* is the amount you earn *before* the money for taxes, health care, retirement plans, and other deductions or contributions are taken out.

Calculate your monthly debt payment using the table below.

TYPE OF DEBT	LENDER	MONTHLY PAYMENT
		$
		$
		$
		$
		$
		$
		$
		$
		$

TOTAL $_____

Helpful Hint: Your total amounts owed are not part of your DTI, but it's always helpful to start keeping track of your total debt because you will need it later on in this workbook!

My monthly debt payment is $_____.

My gross monthly income is $_____.

Helpful Hint: Not sure about your gross monthly income? Try checking your pay stub! Not there? Salaried employees can divide their annual salary by 12.

Hourly employees' gross monthly income can vary, but you can use the formula of (Hourly Pay) × (Weekly Hours Worked) × 52 ÷ 12 to figure out an estimate of your monthly pay.

Let's break that down. If you earn $15 an hour and work 35 hours a week, it'd be ($15) × (35), which equals $525 a week. Then $525 × 52 (the weeks in a year) equals $27,300. You divide that by 12 months and get $2,275 as your gross monthly pay.

Now plug in your personal information and calculate your DTI.

$$\frac{\text{(Monthly debt payments \$_____)}}{\text{(Gross monthly income \$_____)}} = \text{\$_____}$$

Finally, we're going to convert that number into a percentage by simply hitting "× 100" on the calculator. For example ($500 ÷ $2,000) = 0.25. Then 0.25 × 100 = 25%.

My debt-to-income ratio is _____%.

NET WORTH

Your net worth provides a bird's-eye view of your financial situation. It gives a snapshot of your situation at a moment in time by calculating the difference between everything you have and everything you owe. It also helps track your progress toward big financial goals—like having enough for retirement or becoming a millionaire. Like I said, *big* financial goals!

Your net worth is one of the easiest financial calculations to perform. Just don't let a negative number shatter your self-worth! Again, this is just a moment in time. It's not your forever financial situation and it's certainly changeable.

Yes, it is possible to have a negative net worth. In fact, it's fairly common for many people in their twenties to early thirties as they work to pay off student loans and other debts they might have amassed.

Here's the simple formula:

(Total Assets) – (Total Liabilities) = Net Worth

Total assets are more than just your bank accounts and investments. You should also include valuable property like jewelry, paintings, collectibles (oh, Beanie Babies, how I thought you'd be worth something!), and the market value of any real estate or vehicles you own.

Total liabilities include anything you owe like student loans, auto loans, mortgage, credit card debt, even a pending Venmo charge for your friend's birthday dinner or that money you borrowed from your parents a few months ago.

EXERCISE
LET'S CALCULATE YOUR NET WORTH

In the asset table, write down the current balances or current market value of property you own. In the liabilities table, write down all of your outstanding debts.

ASSET	AMOUNT
Home (or any real estate)	$
Retirement accounts	$
Savings accounts	$
Car	$
Art	$
Jewelry	$
Collectibles	$
Other _____	$
Other _____	$

TOTAL $_____

LIABILITY	AMOUNT
Mortgage(s)	$
Auto loan(s)	$
Personal loan(s)	$
Student loans	$
Credit card debt	$
Family/Friend loan	$
Other _____	$
Other _____	$
Other _____	$

TOTAL $_____

Your Net Worth

(Total Assets $_____) − (Total Liabilities $_____) = $_____

HOW MUCH TO SAVE FOR RETIREMENT

Before you start to wrap your mind around retirement planning, I want you to take a few minutes to let yourself daydream about your future. Put on a favorite song, close your eyes, take some deep breaths, and just think about these questions:

What would your dream retirement look like?

What type of life do you want to have as you age?

Where would you live?

What does your home look like?

What would you do day-to-day?

Don't let your inner critic tell you something isn't possible. Tell it to kindly shut up and truly just let your mind dream up your ideal retirement.

EXERCISE
DREAM RETIREMENT

Now write it down.

My dream retirement would be:

_____.

_____.

_____.

_____ .

_____ .

_____ .

_____ .

_____ .

_____ .

_____ .

Great, you've got a vision of what you want. Now it's time for Current You to put in the work so Future You gets that dream retirement!

Speaking of Current You, how is that retirement account looking? I want specifics, so go look it up by logging into your 401(k)/403(b) or IRA account(s).

On _____/_____/20_____, my retirement account(s) was worth $_____.

Don't be ashamed if you just wrote down $0. You're starting right now and that's okay. You're still going to set yourself up for secure retirement.

*Did You Know: We use the wrong language when we say "save for retirement." You shouldn't be saving. You should be **investing** for retirement. I will often default to the common language of "save for retirement" in this workbook because it's familiar, but just know your money should be invested, not sitting in cash in your 401(k)/403(b) or IRA.*

THE COST OF RETIREMENT

One of the biggest struggles with retirement planning is trying to figure out how much you need. It's not easy to figure out because there is so much to consider, like:

- Cost of a home (is a house paid off and you're paying property taxes and upkeep or are you renting?)

- Utilities

- Your regular monthly spend (e.g., grocery shopping)

- Insurance premiums

- Potential medical issues

- Caring for family members

- The overall kind of lifestyle you'd want to have

Because it's not easy to figure out on our own, we tend to crave benchmarks to indicate how we're doing.

EXERCISE
RETIREMENT BENCHMARKS

Listen, I'm really not a fan of benchmarks when it comes to things like retirement. I understand why they can be helpful, but they also run the risk of being really demoralizing too. But I'm also realistic and know that a lot of you reading this are screaming, "Give me the benchmark!" Listen to yourself. If this is going to bum you out because you just wrote $0 for your retirement account balance or because you're just sensitive that way, then SKIP THIS! Go to the next exercise, "How Do You Stack Up?," on page 35.

Last chance to skip this section . . .

Okay, still here?

RETIREMENT "SAVINGS" (INVESTMENTS) BENCHMARK GUIDE [1]

AGE	RATIO
25	0.2:1
30	0.6–0.8:1
35	1.6–1.8:1
45	3–4:1
55	8–10:1
65	16–20:1

You might be thinking, "Uhhh . . . what does that mean?"

Here's how to decode the table. Start with the ratio in the right column. You'll see something like 0.2:1. The 0.2 number in the ratio indicates how many times your salary you should have saved by the age in the left-hand column. The 1 represents one year's worth of salary. So at age 25, you should have saved 0.2 times your annual salary. Well, really you should have 0.2 of your salary. The "times" comes into play more in your forties.

For example, let's say you're 30 and earn $75,000 a year. Your formula is 0.6–0.8 (aka 60%–80%): That means you should have between $45,000–$60,000 in your retirement account by 30. In case it's been a minute since you had to do this kind of math, all I did was ($75,000 × 0.60 = $45,000 and $75,000 × 0.80 = $60,000).

Benchmark age: I'm _____ years old and should have $_____ in my retirement account.

Current retirement balance: I currently have $_____ in my retirement account.

This is not the be-all and end-all of retirement benchmarks. You'll find that there is quite a bit of variation in what experts and financial institutions recommend. But it's within the general ballpark and perhaps even a little on the high side—which I find helpful since it's better to be overprepared for retirement. Again, it is important to remember that a benchmark should not be demoralizing. Being off the trajectory of your benchmark, especially if a recent life or career change has happened, doesn't mean you've screwed everything up or that you'll never successfully retire. It's just a one-size-fits-all recommendation and it might not actually be your size. You can use it as motivation or inspiration to push yourself or you can get excited for our "Build Your Own Benchmark" section coming up!

EXERCISE
HOW DO YOU STACK UP?

Benchmarks, formulas, and ratios are great, but checklists are even better. Who doesn't love crossing something off a to-do list? Reflecting on your mental homework with psychological roadblocks from chapter 2 and using all the knowledge you just soaked up in this chapter, let's combine them all to see exactly where you measure up.

The checklists below serve as a scorecard to figure out if you're a "Participation Trophy" kind of person with your money or a "Gold Star" earner. You might even be on top of your finances enough to earn yourself a "You're Going Viral" award. Let's just hope you aren't a "Living in Your Parents' Basement Forever" kind of person. But if that's you, don't worry. We'll get you working toward your own place by the end of this workbook!

Get out your pen and check the statements that apply to you.

You're Living in Your Parents' Basement Forever

❏ You don't have a savings account.

❏ Your credit score is below 650.

❏ You're underemployed but making no effort to remedy the situation, or you keep quitting full-time jobs because they aren't fulfilling.

❏ You're carrying a balance on a credit card (or several) and paying the minimum due when you remember.

❏ You probably got this workbook as a gift and just happened to flip to this page at random and thought this sounded like you.

You Get a Participation Trophy, but There's Still Work to Do

❑ You've taken a stab at creating a budget.

❑ You always pay at least the minimum on your credit card and most of the time a little bit above the minimum.

❑ You have a 650+ credit score.

❑ You pay the minimum on your non-credit-card debts.

❑ You probably think about creating a get-out-of-debt plan, but then binge-watch the latest Netflix show instead.

❑ You contribute enough to your 401(k) to get the match from your employer.

❑ You were motivated enough to pick up this workbook and begin taking some steps toward taking control (which is a great start!).

You Get a Financial Gold Star!

❑ You have a budget.

❑ You contribute at least 2% above what's needed to get the match on an employer-matched retirement plan.

❑ If an employer-sponsored retirement account—such as a 401(k)—isn't an option, then you're maxing out an IRA.

❑ You've built a 700+ credit score.

❑ You check your credit reports once a year.

❑ You pay off credit cards on time and in full + keep the utilization ratio (amount of total available credit you use) at 30% or less.

❑ You created and started an actionable plan to pay down any debt and are sticking to it by paying above the minimum due on all debts.

❑ You have three months of living expenses in an emergency savings fund if you're debt-free OR have at least one month's worth of bare essential expenses saved if you're prioritizing debt repayment.

You're Going Viral

❑ You have a budget.

❑ You do a monthly net worth update.

❑ You're maxing out your 401(k) and/or IRA.

❑ You have a deadline to be debt-free accompanied by an actionable plan for how to get there.

❑ You're paying double the minimum amount due on your loans each month.

❑ You have a 750+ credit score.

❑ You check your credit reports from all three bureaus each year.

❑ You have at least six months of living expenses in an emergency savings fund if you're debt-free OR you have at least one month of living expenses saved if you're prioritizing the debt payoff.

❑ You pay off credit cards on time and in full + keep utilization ratio (amount of total available credit you use) in the single digits.

❑ You've started investing outside of retirement accounts.

Where do you see the most check marks? _____

No matter where you stack up right now, you're going to be headed toward "Going Viral" (for a good reason!) by the end of this workbook.

EXERCISE
BUILD YOUR OWN BENCHMARK

We crave a benchmark, but personal finance is *personal*. Instead of comparing yourself to total strangers, let's focus on the comparison that matters: how Current You is doing compared to Past You.

In this exercise, you'll create your own "benchmarks" to be able to come back and reflect on that progress.

Emergency Fund

I will sleep more soundly at night if I have _____ months of living expenses saved up.

Currently, I have _____ months of living expenses saved.

In one year, on _____/_____/20_____, I will have at least _____ more months saved.

Emergency Fund Progress Tracker

You can rip the next page out of the workbook and hang it where you'll see it on a regular basis and be motivated to track your progress!

EMERGENCY FUND TRACKER

Each coin represents:

$ _____ amount toward my goal of $ _____ .

Color in the coins each time you make progress toward your goal.

Net Worth

My net worth on _____/_____/20_____ is $_____.

Don't come back to fill this in for at least a year!

My net worth on _____/_____/20_____ is $_____.

Retirement

Before you worry about many decades in the future, let's focus on what you can contribute to your retirement account this year.

I will contribute $_____ to my retirement account by December 31, 20_____ (fill in this year).

Now take that number and divide it by 12.

($_____) ÷ 12 = $_____ per month that I commit to putting into my 401(k)/IRA this year. (Of course, you might not be reading this in January, so you can always modify your division to the number of months remaining in the year and then do this exercise again on January 1 of next year!)

BACK TO THINKING about Way-in-the-Future You. Create customized goals based on your current retirement account balance. DO NOT flip back to see where it "should be." Just focus on what feels right for you.

AGE	PERSONAL GOAL
25	$
30	$
35	$
40	$
45	$
50	$

Next up, we're going to tackle that dreaded B-word. I know you might be tempted to skip this, because budget, gross, but don't! It isn't going to be nearly as painful as you think.

- -

GET YOUR FINANCIAL LIFE TOGETHER CHECK-IN

What is your biggest takeaway (or aha moment) from this chapter?

_____ .

_____ .

_____ .

What feels the most overwhelming about this chapter?

_____ .

_____ .

_____ .

Why does it feel so overwhelming to you in this moment?

_____.

_____.

_____.

Based on what you just learned, write down one actionable step you can take this week to improve your financial life.

_____.

_____.

_____.

Chapter 4

Dealing with the Dreaded B-Word

OH, BUDGETS. An often reviled term for many. Truth be told, budgets simply get a bad rap. But I probably don't have to tell you that. Instead, how about you share your feelings?

How do you feel about budgets? (What words come to mind when you hear "budget"?)

_____.

_____.

Have you ever used a budget successfully (even for a short period)?

_____.

_____.

What worked or what didn't?

_____.

_____.

A QUICK REBRAND

I'm going to take a guess that some of your answers to that exercise were at least a little bit negative. Most people don't have positive feelings about budgets because the budgeting styles they used felt restrictive or became frustrating.

There has been a movement within personal finance to rebrand how we talk about budgets. Instead of using the dreaded B-word, you can reframe it as a "spending plan." It sounds more fun, right? Ultimately, that's all a budget is. **It's a plan about how you're going to spend/save/invest your money.** Even if you technically don't have a defined budget, well, you still do budget your money. It's just a chaotic one that leaves you feeling like you don't know where your money went or that you never have enough.

When deployed correctly, a budget can help you feel in control of your finances. This is even true when you're earning a modest amount and feeling overwhelmed about your income compared to expenses.

Focusing first on what you value and want to prioritize is a key element in ensuring your budget doesn't feel restrictive and instead feels like a spending plan.

WHAT DO YOU VALUE?

Think about your monthly spending habits. What do you think you spend your money on?

_____.

_____.

Is your spending in alignment with what you say you value? Write down what you value most.

_____.

_____.

EXERCISE
CHECK YOURSELF

Step 1: Print out the last three to six months of your credit card and bank statements.

Step 2: Get a few different-colored highlighters.

Step 3: Assign colors to categories that cover what you said you value and be sure to include "necessity" as one. For example, your categories might be necessity (e.g., groceries, shelter, debt payments, insurance, etc.), investing, entertainment, dining out, travel, charitable giving. Also assign colors to transactions that fall outside of your value sets.

Step 4: Begin reading through your bank and credit card statements and highlight each transaction with the appropriate color.

Step 5: Evaluate your colorful bank and credit card statements to see if your spending, saving, and investing patterns are actually in alignment with what you said you value.

Are you in alignment?

YES / NO

If you answered no, what is out of whack?

_____.

_____.

What is causing you to spend in a way that isn't in alignment with your values?

_____.

_____.

Now that you have those bank and credit card statements handy, let's talk about where your money is going every month!

KNOW YOUR CASH FLOW

The personal cash flow equation is simple:

(How much is coming in) − (How much is going out) = Cash Flow

You earn $3,000 a month in take-home pay and your monthly spend is $2,700; then you have $300 left to spend or put toward other financial goals.

If your cash flow number is negative, then it's time to do a hard edit of your monthly expenses and see what you can cut. In tandem, you can work on increasing your income by either negotiating your salary or picking up a side hustle (or both!).

There is one strange wrinkle to personal cash flow, and that is how we categorize retirement contributions and other savings and investments. Technically, you would think of that as "going out" simply in the sense that it's not money available for you to spend in the month. Your retirement contribution may also already be accounted for because you contribute before money hits your bank account and therefore doesn't come out of your take-home pay.

It's okay to get $0 when you run your cash flow if you're including savings and investment contributions. A negative number means you're overspending. A positive number means you can put more money toward financial goals or spend in other ways.

EXERCISE
DETERMINE YOUR CASH FLOW

My monthly take-home pay is $_____.

Helpful Hint: Cash flow planning for a budget is typically based on a month's worth of income and spending. So what should you do about annual costs like subscriptions or fees? Personally, I add them all up and divide by 12 so those costs are factored into my monthly budget and I always have money set aside to pay the bill with no disruption to my overall budget.

MONTHLY EXPENSE	COST
Rent/mortgage	$
HOA/co-op/condo fee	$
Electric (you can use an average for variable costs like electric)	$
Internet/cable	$
Water	$
Gas	$
Cell phone	$
Child/pet care	$
Insurance premiums	$
Medicine	$
Transportation (gas/public transit pass)	$
Auto loan	$

Student loans	$
Credit card debt	$
Monthly payment of annual fees	$
Household goods (e.g., toilet paper and cleaning supplies)	$
Beauty products	$
Beauty services	$
Food	$
Entertainment	$
Retirement	$
Investing/savings goals	$
Charitable giving	$
Other _____	$
Other _____	$
Other _____	$
TOTAL	$

(Your monthly take home pay) – (Your monthly expenses/savings/investments) = Cash Flow

($_____) – ($_____) = $_____

PICKING THE RIGHT STYLE FOR YOU

There are myriad ways you can take control of your money, which is why it's imperative you select one that works for both your financial situation and for your personality. The hands-on, type A people among us may prefer the "Tracking Every Penny" option to get a daily and detailed overview of their financial situations. If you're more laid back yet money conscious, you may prefer a percentage-based budget to know where to allocate funds without focusing on monitoring each swipe of the credit or debit card.

In this chapter, we'll review different budgeting styles to help you decide which one is right for you or which one to switch to so you feel empowered instead of overwhelmed. We're going to overview only four budgets in this chapter, but just know there are many more out there, or you can use elements from these budgets to inspire your own system. My current budget is a hybrid of the Zero-Sum Budget with influences of the envelope method and percentage budgeting!

Tracking Every Penny

Do you tend to get struck with that feeling of "What the hell did I spend my money on?!" each month? Then the "Tracking Every Penny" method is for you—at least for a while.

The name says it all: You're going to record every financial transaction you make, down to the penny. You keep a meticulous record of every financial transaction instead of just saying, "I have $200 to spend this week," because you're ultimately looking for insights. You want to know not only how much you spent, but what you spent it on. Unfortunately, debit and credit card transactions don't always offer that insight, especially at a store like Target. You just see that you went to Target and might not remember what you actually purchased.

An additional bonus element to Tracking Every Penny is to note your emotional state when making a purchase. For those who struggle with compulsive shopping or generally spending money as a reaction to a heightened emotional state, it can help provide critical insights to analyze later.

What are the top five ways you think you spend your money each month?

1. _____

2. _____

3. _____

4. _____

5. _____

After at least two weeks (but a month is better) of doing the "Tracking Every Penny" budget, come back here and write down, in order, the top five ways you actually spend your money.

1. _____

2. _____

3. _____

4. _____

5. _____

Personally, I think the easiest way to track every penny is via the notes app on your phone. Then if you want to level up, you can transfer that information to a Google doc or Excel spreadsheet later on to make it easier to analyze.

DATE	PURCHASE	COST	EMOTIONS
April 5, 2023	Latte	$5	Caffeine deprived, needed a break from work, or wanted the social interaction because I work from home

Transferring the data over to another spreadsheet also enables you to add additional categories for you to filter and track your spending habits, such as money spent on food, bills, debt, pets, clothes, and entertainment. Below, you'll see "category" was added, which could enable you to easily filter in spreadsheets.

DATE	PURCHASE	CATEGORY	COST	EMOTIONS
April 5, 2023	Latte	Food	$5	Caffeine deprived, needed a break from work, or wanted the social interaction because I work from home

The goal here is never to shame yourself for spending behaviors, but instead to see if you are truly spending in alignment with your self-proclaimed values. I for one actually do value a latte. It's one of my favorite drinks and I don't have the equipment to make one at home. It helps break up some monotony in my work-from-home day. Plus, I can walk the dog to my favorite neighborhood coffee shops (one of which is a dog café, where she gets socialization time too!).

However, you might find that you're consistently spending on quick takeout that is more of a reaction to exhaustion instead of actually wanting that particular food. Or maybe you've gotten into a rut of routinely spending a few bucks on mindless purchases that you don't actually need.

I encouraged my first postcollege roommate to participate in this practice when she was looking to free up some additional funds in her budget in order to pay for a class she wanted to take. Within a week she came to me dumbfounded, saying, "I spend nearly $20 a week buying bottled water!" It had become a mindless practice to buy a bottle of water at Starbucks during her workday because she wanted a break from work. Those overpriced bottles added up quickly. Just carrying around a reusable bottle of water at work and going for a walk instead of a trip to Starbucks added $80 a month back into her budget.

The Envelope System

The Envelope System dictates how much you can spend in certain categories. Then you shove cash into envelopes and pay for each transaction using cash out of the associated envelope.

Let's call a spade a spade. This method is dated. Well, the original application of this method is dated. The principle remains solid: You never borrow from one envelope to beef up another. Once you're tapped out in one envelope, then you're done being able to spend in that category for the remainder of the month. The traditional approach of using cash also helped you physically watch money dwindle down.

In order for this to work effectively in today's world, where a lot of our bills are paid digitally, it makes more sense to focus only on monthly household and personal spending for your envelopes. Categories like groceries, transportation, entertainment, etc. Your rent/mortgage, utility bills, student loans, and auto loans are all being paid online and not with cash.

How much do you have remaining after paying off your big bills like housing, debt payments, and utilities and putting money into your retirement fund?

$_____ *in remaining funds each month.*

What do you spend that money on each month?

1. _____

2. _____

3. _____

4. _____

5. _____

Now assign a dollar amount from your remaining funds to each of those categories.

1. _____

2. _____

3. _____

4. _____

5. _____

In a true envelope system, you would get the appropriate number of envelopes and write the category on the outside and then distribute the cash accordingly. You might want to try that for a month or so, but it's also okay if you'd prefer a digital option. Goodbudget and Mvelopes are both apps for a digital envelope system.

The Power of Multiple Bank Accounts

The traditional envelope system is no longer a budget I use, but there is something powerful in having either multiple bank accounts *or* buckets within your bank accounts. Certain banks have features that allow you to set up savings or spending buckets within your accounts. All the money will still be housed in one account, but you get the visual aid of seeing that $X is for this goal and $X is for that goal.

Personally, I also use multiple bank accounts for different parts of my budget. I have a checking account specifically for bills. A checking account just for my personal spending. Then I have savings accounts that are segmented with the buckets to account for different goals. The separation of my personal spending money from money for my bills helps make sure there is always money to pay rent, utilities, insurance premiums, annual fees, etc.

In essence, this was a way to digitally carry over some of the principles of the envelope budget into the digital age as I moved on to other, less restrictive budgeting styles.

Helpful Hint: Some personal finance gurus will advise—or rather mandate— that you not have a fun fund while you are paying down debt. I'm a more practical millennial who would prefer you don't yo-yo-diet with your finances. Having a small fun fund you can use to make a splurge purchase or go out with your friends ($50 or less each month if you're paying off debt) sometimes will keep you from falling off the wagon and blowing your budget out of the water due to sheer frustration at having to live a fun-deprived hermitlike lifestyle.

Percentage-Based Budget

One of the more effective and less stringent budgeting methods—the Percentage-Based Budget—often outlines three main categories for your cash:

1. Fixed costs, aka necessities (50 percent)
2. Financial goals (20 percent)
3. Wants or flexible spending (30 percent)

In an ideal version of the universe, these three groups are easily funded only by your income. Twenty percent of the money goes toward saving and maybe additional debt payments, while 50 percent more than covers your housing, transportation, and minimum debt costs, and the remainder funds your day-to-day living.

In reality, you might be chuckling to yourself at the notion of spending only 50 percent on your fixed expenses, especially if you're sitting in an apartment located in a major city. Your rent alone might be 50 percent of your salary, and that doesn't include paying utilities, taking care of your transportation, and, of course, paying down those student loans.

The idealized version of a Percentage-Based Budget is a great goal, but in the meantime, it's fine to develop your own reasonable percentages for those three major categories. Reasonable is not spending 40 percent on fixed costs, 55 percent on flexible spending, and 5 percent on meeting financial goals. When you create your own percentages, it's also important to reevaluate them as you pay down debt, progress in your career, and increase your available income.

EXERCISE
CREATING YOUR OWN PERCENTAGES

My monthly gross income is: $_____.

_____ % of my monthly income goes to a retirement plan (401[k]/IRA).

My net* monthly income is: $_____.

Fill in how much each of the categories below costs per month:

Housing: $_____

Utilities: $_____

----

* Net is what hits my checking account after paying taxes and contributing to retirement.

Transportation: $_____

Minimum debt payments: $_____

Insurance premiums: $_____

Medicine: $_____

Child/pet care: $_____

Other essentials: $_____

Now add them all up:

Total: $_____

Take that grand total for the cost of your essential living expenses and divide it by your net monthly income and multiply the answer by 100 to get a percentage.

$_____ ÷ $_____ = _____ × 100 = _____ %

This is the percentage you currently spend on necessities.
Subtract that from 100%.

(100%) − (_____ %) = _____ %

This is how much you have left for the "wants" and "financial goals" categories.

Now, keep in mind that if a percentage of your gross income is going toward retirement, then you're already funding some of the "financial goals" category. What you just calculated was based on your net income, so your postretirement contributions income.

Set your realistic goals based on all the information you have right now.

_____ *% goes toward needs.*

_____ *% goes toward financial goals.*

_____ *% goes toward wants.*

Set your idealistic goals based on where you'd like to be in six months.

_____ *% Needs*

_____ *% Wants*

_____ *% Financial Goals*

Zero-Sum Budget

The Zero-Sum Budget operates with a simple principle in mind: Assign every dollar a job so you zero out your money each month. Don't get too excited! It doesn't mean you *spend* all your dollars. Assigning a job includes savings and investing goals.

The black belt of budgeting tactics, the Zero-Sum Budget uses last month's income to pay for this month's expenses. This method is the one to learn if you earn variable income. It's also the foundation for the popular budgeting tool YNAB (You Need a Budget), one of many budgeting apps you could use.

It takes a little time and patience to master, but once you do, it's a powerful way to feel in control, no matter how you earn income, and to aggressively pay off debt and hit savings goals.

Helpful Hint: For my fellow variable-income earners like the self-employed or those who work off commission, consider paying yourself a salary. Doing this revolutionized my budget! All my business income goes into my business account. I then pay myself a consistent salary each month. The business account fattens during boom times, which enables me to still pay myself the same salary in lean earning months.

Step 1: *Know Your Income*

Luckily, you already have this information!

My monthly income is $_____.

Step 2: *Calculate Your Bills and Expenses.*

You've done this already in the cash flow exercise on pages 48 and 49!

Step 3: *Employ Your Dollars.*

Did your cash flow end with a positive number? If so, it's time to assign even those dollars a job! The goal here is to account for all the money you earn each month.

Here's your chance to customize your Zero-Sum Budget by creating categories that are unique to you and filling in how much you're going to spend per month. You might not need to use every category below and you may have others I didn't account for here. Feel free to build your own off this page!

HOUSING COSTS

MONTHLY EXPENSE	COST
	$
	$
	$
	$
	$
	$

TOTAL $_____

UTILITIES

MONTHLY EXPENSE	COST
	$
	$
	$
	$
	$
	$

TOTAL $_____

TRANSPORTATION

MONTHLY EXPENSE	COST
	$
	$
	$
	$
	$
	$

TOTAL $_____

FOOD

MONTHLY EXPENSE	COST
	$
	$
	$
	$
	$
	$

TOTAL $_____

INSURANCE PREMIUMS

MONTHLY EXPENSE	COST
	$
	$
	$
	$
	$
	$

TOTAL $_____

DEBT

MONTHLY EXPENSE	COST
	$
	$
	$
	$
	$
	$

TOTAL $_____

MEDICINE

MONTHLY EXPENSE	COST
	$
	$
	$
	$
	$
	$

TOTAL $_____

HOUSEHOLD GOODS

MONTHLY EXPENSE	COST
	$
	$
	$
	$
	$
	$

TOTAL $_____

SELF-CARE

MONTHLY EXPENSE	COST
	$
	$
	$
	$
	$
	$

TOTAL $_____

CHILDREN/PETS

MONTHLY EXPENSE	COST
	$
	$
	$
	$
	$
	$

TOTAL $_____

ENTERTAINMENT

MONTHLY EXPENSE	COST
	$
	$
	$
	$
	$
	$

TOTAL $_____

SAVINGS/INVESTING GOALS

MONTHLY EXPENSE	COST
	$
	$
	$
	$
	$
	$

TOTAL $_____

CHARITABLE GIVING

MONTHLY EXPENSE	COST
	$
	$
	$
	$
	$
	$

TOTAL $_____

MISCELLANEOUS

Other monthly payments you make (e.g., supporting family members). This section can also include breaking annual costs into monthly chunks to save up for when that payment is due or setting aside money for unexpected—but expected—costs like new tires on your car.

MONTHLY EXPENSE	COST
	$
	$
	$
	$
	$
	$

TOTAL $_____

REMAINING FUNDS	$

Step 4: *Aim to Get a Month Ahead (or More).*

The money you earned last month is what should be used to pay your bills. I know that can sound really stressful at first or almost impossible. It's not. As you focus on spending within your means and being in total control over where your money goes each month, you'll find you can put yourself in the position to use last month's income to pay for this month's expenses. You could create a category that funds your "month ahead" by slowly saving up a month's worth of expenses. This concept is fundamentally what it means to break the paycheck-to-paycheck cycle.

Step 5: *Always Run the Numbers and Adjust Accordingly.*

This budget is hands on, which means you need to be checking in weekly, perhaps even daily as you work toward getting a month ahead. It's imperative you know exactly how much you earned last month, so you can adjust your categories accordingly. This is why the Zero-Sum Budget is ideal for freelancers and helps destroy paycheck-to-paycheck living.

Just be sure the categories you're adjusting are the nonessentials. If you're making $1,000 less in June than you did in May, your entertainment budget should be taking the hit before your savings or debt-slaying categories.

YOUR BUDGET SHOULD CHANGE AS YOUR LIFE CHANGES

Picking the right budget (or spending plan) for you will probably take some time. That's okay! Test one for a few months, and if it doesn't fit, try another. You can absolutely learn how to create an effective budget for yourself. A big part is to not get too restrictive and certainly don't berate yourself when the occasional budget buster occurs.

Finally, remember that it's okay for your budget to change over time. **In fact, our budgets should evolve as our lives change.** The budget I use now looks nothing like the budget I used a decade ago because my life and financial situation are different!

The ultimate goal is to feel in control, which is why having a budget should empower you in your financial life and not stress you out.

- -

Get Your Financial Life Together Check-In

What is your biggest takeaway (or aha moment) from this chapter?

_____.

_____.

_____.

What feels the most overwhelming about this chapter? (It's okay if the answer is: "Crap, I actually do need to budget. . . .")

_____.

_____.

_____.

Why does it feel so overwhelming to you in this moment?

_____.

_____.

_____.

Based on what you just learned, write down one actionable step you can take this week to improve your financial life.

_____.

_____.

_____.

Chapter 5

Picking the Right Financial Products

HAVE YOU EVER questioned how and why you use the financial products you're using? If you haven't, well, you should.

How did you pick your bank?

_____.

For many people, the answer is along the lines of:

- There's a branch near my house.

- It's what my parents use.

- That bank was advertised on my college campus.

How long have you been with your bank?

_____.

When was the last time you did research to see if there was a better option available?

_____.

All too often, the answer to that question is a resounding *never*.

No matter your level of financial know-how and expertise, we can all go on autopilot by just staying with what we know or what our parents use when it comes to actually picking our financial products—checking and savings accounts, credit cards, and even your lenders for auto loans, personal loans, or mortgages. Our parents had fewer options available to them at our age, so they couldn't shop around in the same way we can today. But thanks to the Internet and the subsequent rise of Internet-only banks, as well as online comparison tools that help you find the right financial products for you, you don't have to use financial products just because Mom and Dad did or because there's a branch on your block.

Let's do some exercises to help you figure out if you're using the best financial products for you and discuss how to find alternatives.

This chapter is going to focus on checking and savings accounts. Chapter 7 focuses on the proper use of credit cards and how to pick the right one for you.

EXERCISE
AUDITING YOUR FINANCIAL PRODUCTS: DO YOU KNOW WHAT YOU'RE USING?

There is a very good chance that you signed up for a checking or savings account without really paying attention to the quality of the product. Let's start with analyzing your current financial products in the following categories:

- **Bank:** Self-explanatory. Just write down the bank you use for that product. It's okay if there are multiple banks (e.g., I use three banks and have checking and savings accounts at all of them).

- **Monthly Fee & ATM Fee:** How much are you being charged or would you be charged each month to have that account? How much does it cost for you to use an ATM that's not associated with your bank?

- **Fine Print:** Many banks will waive the monthly fee *if* you jump through some hoops. For example, the $12 monthly fee will be waived if you have a minimum daily balance of $1,500 or a qualifying direct deposit of $1,000 or more during the month.

- **Interest Rate:** How much is the bank paying you in interest to have a checking or savings account there? This is sometimes written as APY (annual percentage yield).

- **Overdraft:** Write down how much the fee is if/when you go overdraft.

- **Overdraft Protection:** How much does it cost to use overdraft protection? Some banks charge a fee to move your money from one account to another to cover an overdraft.

- **Additional Benefits:** Are there any other gimmicks (e.g., rounding up change) that your bank uses?

Helpful Hint: Not sure where to find this information? You have a few options:

1. *Log in to your account and search for "account details."*

2. *If "account details" doesn't share all the information you need, then try just Googling the type of account. For example, [Bank Name] Classic Checking. Banks do have to disclose fee information. It might take a little bit of digging, but you can usually find it on the page promoting various products.*

3. *Call up customer service. I know, I know—who wants to deal with calling a bank's customer service! But that is a last resort if you can't find out the information another way.*

Fill out your information on the following grids.

CHECKING ACCOUNTS

BANK	MONTHLY FEE & ATM FEE	FINE PRINT	INTEREST RATE	OVERDRAFT FEE	OVERDRAFT PROTECTION FEE
	$		%	$	$
	$		%	$	$
	$		%	$	$
	$		%	$	$

SAVINGS ACCOUNTS

BANK	MONTHLY FEE	FINE PRINT	INTEREST RATE	ADDITIONAL BENEFITS
	$		%	
	$		%	
	$		%	
	$		%	
	$		%	
	$		%	

Did You Know: FDIC insurance is a critical part of vetting any bank you plan to use. The Federal Deposit Insurance Corporation (FDIC) insures depositors' money up to a set amount, so even if a bank fails, the insured sum is protected. To be clear, this does not cover investments or life insurance policies. As of 2022, your money is insured up to $250,000 per insured bank for each account ownership category. To be clear, it doesn't mean per account, e.g., having multiple checking or savings accounts at the same bank. It's $250,00 total per institution.

EXERCISE
AM I USING THE WRONG FINANCIAL PRODUCTS?

Read the statements below and check the box if it applies to your bank account(s).

❏ I pay (or have had to pay) a monthly fee for checking and/or savings.

❏ I've never paid a fee, but my bank will charge me a monthly fee if I don't have a minimum balance or get a certain amount in direct deposits.

❏ My bank charges me when I use another bank's ATM and doesn't reimburse me the fee charged by the other bank. (For example: You bank with ABC Bank, but you're traveling and the city you're in only has XYZ Banks. You need to get cash out and go to an XYZ Bank ATM. Your ABC Bank charges you $2.50 for using another bank's ATM and XYZ Bank charges you $3 to use its ATM because you aren't a customer.)

❏ I have paid hefty overdraft fees (or my bank would charge a big overdraft fee).

❏ I use overdraft protection and get charged a fee when my own money is moved from one account to another to cover the possible overdraft.

❏ The interest rate (APY) on my savings account is between 0.01% to 0.05%.

If you checked any of these boxes, then you should consider switching!

I AM USING THE WRONG FINANCIAL PRODUCTS. NOW WHAT?

Now it's time to make the big switch. You're going to do some research to find better options and then migrate your accounts over.

Here's What You Should Expect from Checking and Savings Accounts (Check It Off If This Applies to Your Account)

❏ No annual fee

❏ No monthly maintenance fee

❏ No minimum amount required to avoid fees

❏ No overdraft protection fee

❏ No fee charged when you use an ATM outside of your bank's network, plus a reimbursement of the fee levied against you by the ATM you're using. At bare minimum: a certain amount of ATM fees reimbursed per billing cycle, such as $10 worth.

❏ Bonus points if there's no cost to replace lost or stolen debit cards

❏ A savings account should offer you more than 0.01% to 0.05% APY.

HOW TO FIND BETTER FINANCIAL PRODUCTS

Checking and Savings Accounts

Internet-only banks often provide the most competitive deals, but traditional brick-and-mortar banks have started to get more competitive. You may hear Internet-only banks called online banks, which is also true, but Internet-only is more accurate. These are the financial institutions with no or very few brick-and-mortar locations. They are perfectly safe so long as they are FDIC-insured institutions.

Google can be your best friend when searching for these banks, but some notable checking account options that have been on the market for at least several years include:

- Ally

- USAA (you do need military affiliation)

- Charles Schwab's High-Yield Investor Checking*

- Fidelity Cash Management Account*

However, big banks are starting to take notice of these Internet-only competitors, and some are adapting to the new banking experience. Capital One offers the Capital One 360 checking account, which is a no-fee account so long as you use a Capital One ATM machine.

However, if you deal primarily in cash for your job or tend to receive a lot of cash (e.g., tips as a bartender), this may not be a valid option for you. Many Internet-only bank accounts do not provide a solution for the cash-deposit dilemma. Capital One 360 does offer the ability to deposit cash at select ATM machines.

Don't sleep on your local credit union either! Most of this discussion has been about banks that are nationwide, but your community credit union may offer competitive financial products too, especially for loans. It's worth checking out the terms and fine print of savings and checking accounts at your local credit union. Another option is to explore credit unions that offer memberships to those outside of its local community. For example, I was able to get a membership to a credit union by making a small donation to a charitable organization the credit union supports.

Where to Do the Research

You should absolutely do your own research. Google can be your best friend, but the websites below are also reputable places that rank products.

- MagnifyMoney

- NerdWallet

---

* These accounts usually require having a brokerage account. There is a Fidelity Bank, but this refers to Fidelity Investments.

- Bankrate

- Credit Karma

Just keep in mind that most of these companies pay the bills by earning referral fees from the financial institutions they send customers to. Because of this, some of these sites will rank products based on how much they get paid and not what is necessarily the best fit for you. **Read through reviews before making any selections on a financial product, and read the fine print (or at least skim details) before applying.**

CHALLENGE
TIME TO SWITCH

I need to switch the following checking accounts/savings accounts because I'm being charged unnecessary fees.

_____.

_____.

_____.

_____.

After doing my research, I'm going to switch to:

_____.

_____.

_____.

_____.

Before I switch, I'm going to double-check for any and all automatic bill payments connected to my account. I will update those payments with my new bank account information _before_ I close my old bank account. Those payments are:

_____.

_____.

_____.

_____.

Helpful Hint: Monthly payments are easy to find, but print out bank statements from the last six months to a year and scan those to look for auto payments that are semiannual or annual.

Extra Credit: Take customer service for a test drive before you commit to switching! Give them a call and check for wait times, how frustrating it is to get access to a real human and not a robo menu, and how helpful you find the representative. I give brownie points to companies that tell you what the wait time will be and offer to call you back instead of leaving you on hold forever.

KEY TAKEAWAYS TO NOTE WHEN CHOOSING YOUR FINANCIAL PRODUCTS

→ Make sure your bank has FDIC insurance.

→ You don't need to pay unnecessary fees on a checking or savings account like maintenance, annual fees, minimums, and overdraft protection. There are ways to avoid those.

→ Your savings account should be earning an interest rate that's the highest available on the market. For example, in 2018 that was 2.00% APY, in 2020 it was 0.50% APY, and in 2022 it rose again to higher than 2.00% APY. Savings rates change, but the common offer of 0.01% is a joke—both you and your money deserve better.

- -

GET YOUR FINANCIAL LIFE TOGETHER CHECK-IN

What is your biggest takeaway (or aha moment) from this chapter?

_____.

_____.

_____.

What feels the most overwhelming about this chapter?

_____.

_____.

_____.

Why does it feel so overwhelming to you in this moment?

_____.

_____.

_____.

Based on what you just learned, write down one actionable step you can take this week to improve your financial life.

_____.

_____.

_____.

Chapter 6

Credit Reports and Scores: The Report Card for Life

THERE ARE TWO popular myths about credit scores and reports.

1. It's a "debt score."
2. You don't need a credit score because you shouldn't be in debt.

Here is me giving a hugely dramatic eye roll.

First of all, you don't need to be in debt in order to build a strong credit score and history. In fact, you can go without ever paying a penny toward interest or debt and still get an 800+ credit score.

Second, it's not just lenders who use your credit score.

WHY CREDIT SCORES AND REPORTS MATTER AND WHO USES THEM

You may think it's the credit card companies, mortgage lenders, and car dealers of the world who would be most interested in your credit score and report. Unfortunately, that just isn't so. The reach of a credit report and score extends far beyond your attempt to get someone to believe you're qualified to borrow money.

The credit report and score is used as a way to judge your levels of responsibility—or really gauge just how well you're succeeding at adulting.

Other people or companies who may use your credit score and/or credit report include:

- A landlord

- Insurance companies

- A potential employer (but you usually do have to agree)

- Utility companies

Did You Know: You may have heard that employers check your credit score, but this isn't true. Employers pull the credit report, which doesn't actually come with the credit score. It can be used to get a sense of how responsible you are or to verify your identity.

Think of a strong, healthy credit score and report as an insurance policy on your financial life.

Sure, in an ideal world, we'd never have to borrow money. We could all pay for a house or car or child's education in cash. The reality is, that isn't the case for most people. You may need to borrow money at some point, and a strong credit score not only unlocks access to borrowing, but it also means a lower interest rate. Plus, in competitive rental markets, it can become extremely difficult to get a landlord to approve you without a strong credit score.

Disclaimer

Okay, there's something a bit frustrating when you talk about credit scores and reports. There are so many different credit-scoring models and more than one credit-scoring company. For simplicity's sake, this chapter will focus on FICO credit scoring. Other credit-scoring companies are quite close in alignment with FICO. There are also three main credit bureaus, which generate credit reports: Experian, Equifax, and TransUnion.

WHAT'S THE DIFFERENCE BETWEEN MY CREDIT SCORE AND MY CREDIT REPORT?

The credit report contains the information used to generate your credit score. The credit score is the simple, easy-to-understand piece of information we can all use to judge one another, but the report is really what matters most.

Credit reports contain a detailed history of the ways in which you've interacted with credit and debt. It even includes things like applications for loans you might not have gotten. Items that have gone to collections, missed payments, defaulting, or going delinquent on your payments can all be reported and will impact your credit score. Information will stay on your credit report between two to ten years, depending on the item. A loan application will roll off sooner than a bankruptcy.

Your credit report *does not* include your credit score. Credit bureaus (Experian, Equifax, and TransUnion) create credit reports. Companies like FICO and VantageScore use that information to generate your credit scores.

EXERCISE
CHECK YOUR CREDIT REPORT

Under federal law, you are entitled to a free annual copy of your credit report from each credit bureau. There are sometimes modifications to this rule in which you are allowed more access for free. During the pandemic, consumers could get weekly access to their credit reports. You might be tempted to ignore your credit report and focus on just your credit score, but don't! Checking your credit report is an important way to check for identity theft or just a mistake on the part of credit bureaus (especially if you have a common name).

Did You Know: Pulling your own credit report will not hurt your credit score!

You can go to AnnualCreditReport.com for a centralized way to get access to all three credit bureaus (Experian, Equifax, and TransUnion).

Pull at least one of your credit reports right now and check that it is accurate.

Things to Look for on Your Credit Report

- Personal information is accurate including your name, history of addresses, Social Security number, marital status, and employment information.

- The financial products associated with your account are correct (e.g., loans and credit cards).

- Check to see if any loans or financial products on the report are not ones for which you applied. This could indicate identity theft. This would be in the "inquiries" section and/or "credit accounts" section.

- Items reported as in collections, in default, or delinquent. It's possible an item could end up in collections and on your credit report before you even get a call.

⚠️ *Be 100% sure you go to the correct website. There are a lot of scams out there! AnnualCredit-Report.com is vetted by the Federal Trade Commission (FTC). If you have any concerns, you can go to consumer.ftc.gov/articles/free-credit-reports to read more.*

If something isn't right, you can dispute the item directly with the credit bureau. You can also put a fraud alert or credit freeze on your report to minimize an identity thief's access.

UNDERSTANDING YOUR CREDIT SCORE

Your credit score is a number that basically provides a snapshot of what is on your credit report. It's a visual representation of your history as a borrower or user of credit.

Your goal is to be in the 700+ category in order to have access to top-tier financial products.

Here is the general breakdown:

800+: exceptional

750–799: excellent credit

700–749: good credit

640–699: fair

580–639: poor credit

Below 580: bad credit

A *high credit score* will result in low (or lower) interest rates on any money you borrow and therefore save you money over the life of the loan. A *low credit score* will mean high interest rates on loans or potential outright rejection of your loan applications from lenders.

We'll dig into what impacts your credit score soon. But first, let's talk about what is *not* used to determine your credit score.

- Race

- Age

- Religion

- National origin

- Gender

- Marital status

- Employer

- Occupation

- Interest rates you're being charged

- If you're in credit counseling

- Child support or alimony payments

EXERCISE
COLOR ME TO 700+

Take a moment right now to go look up your current credit score.

There are a few free ways you can do this. See if your credit card(s) offer monthly credit score access. If not, you could use Credit Karma, Capital One's CreditWise, American Express's MyCredit Guide, Credit Sesame, or Mint to name a few. You do not need to pay or deal with a free trial.

> *Did You Know: While it's great to get free access to a credit score, we all know nothing is truly free. Be mindful of how your data is being used. Also, most companies offering free credit scores will pitch you recommended financial products. The company usually gets a commission if you choose to use one of those products. The financial products being pitched to you are not always the crème de la crème or the absolute best options for you specifically. Always do your own research!*

As of ____/_____/20_____ my credit score is _____·.

Your goal is to get into the 700+ club, but hey, it's also okay to reach for that coveted 800+ score! Tracking your progress is a powerful tool when it comes to achieving your goals. So let's do just that. Use the next page as a way to color in and track your progress. Keep in mind that it can take a couple years to really rehabilitate a credit score, so don't get discouraged if you don't see quick movement in the early months.

TRACK YOUR PROGRESS

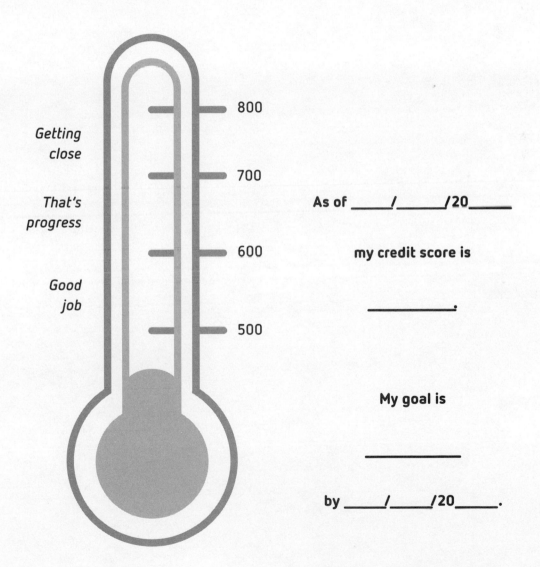

Getting close

That's progress

800

700

As of _____/_____/20_____

Good job

600

500

my credit score is

_____.

My goal is

_____

by _____/_____/20_____.

HOLD UP, I CHECKED MY CREDIT SCORE AND IT SAID "THIN FILE." WTF?!

A thin file can also be the result of no or minimal credit history. You may be in the process of building—or rebuilding—your credit, and there simply isn't enough information on your credit report to generate a score.

Don't panic over your thin file. This isn't the time to start applying for a bunch of credit. Keep steady at using one or two credit cards wisely and making payments on any existing loans. This strategy will build a strong credit history, and you'll have a credit score in no time.

> *Did You Know: Student loans help build your credit score if you pay them on time and never let them default or become delinquent. If you are in college and aren't making payments, your student loans won't be helping you build credit until you graduate and start forking over money each month. The same will go for a loan in deferment. Just having loans in your name isn't enough. The credit bureaus need to see that you're making payments and keeping your loans in good standing.*

One potentially worrisome reason for a thin file could be a mistaken death. If you have years of credit history under your belt and pop up as having a thin file, or one or more of your creditors marked you as deceased on an account. You should pull your credit report immediately. It's not unheard-of for the credit bureaus to mistakenly mark someone who is still roaming the earth as deceased.

Now that you've checked your credit score, let's explore how exactly the credit-scoring models are determining that number.

THE FIVE FACTORS

There are five factors used to determine your credit score.

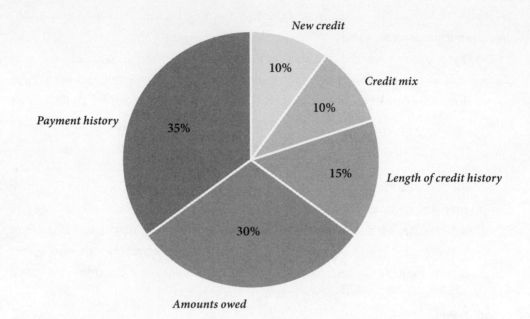

1. **Payment history (35 percent):** What's the best indicator whether or not you'll pay on time in the future? If you've paid on time in the past. Payment history is the most heavily weighted category when calculating your credit score, and the way to keep it strong is to simply make your payments on time each month.

2. **Amounts owed (aka utilization; 30 percent):** Amounts owed often goes by the far-more-exotic name of utilization, the amount of available credit you spend. Your goal should be to spend less than 30 percent of your available credit and single digits are even better. That means, if you have a $1,000 line of credit, then you spend no more than $300. We'll dig more into this in an upcoming exercise.

3. **Length of credit history (15 percent):** This section is easy to handle with a two-step process.

   - Step 1: Use your credit.
   - Step 2: Don't die anytime soon.

   Boom. Nailed it.

   Okay, it may be slightly more nuanced. The third step would be to keep your oldest line of credit alive for at least the early years. If it's a terrible, fee-riddled card with less appeal than going back to using a flip phone, then I give you permission to ditch it, but not until you've secured yourself another credit card with no annual fee.

   An active credit card is the simplest way to keep your length of credit history healthy.

4. **Credit mix (10 percent):** As the name implies, this factor is the diversification of your lines of credit (e.g., having credit cards, an auto loan, some student loans, and a mortgage). You absolutely *do not* need to take on debt just for the sake of this credit-scoring factor. It's only 10 percent of your total score and you can totally build a strong credit score with no debt by using a credit card and paying it off on time and in full.

5. **New credit (10 percent):** Do you keep applying for loans or credit cards? Trying to open a bunch of credit cards quickly or taking on several loans is a red flag to the credit-scoring companies.

Did You Know: It's okay to shop around when planning to take out a loan. If you apply to several loans to check your rate within a 14-day window, then the credit-scoring model will note that you were shopping for a deal and not on a rampage to take on a ton of loans. The behavior will be weighted against your score as such. Don't let the "new credit" factor prevent you from shopping around for the best deal. Credit card applications aren't quite the same, so it's wise not to apply for a bunch of credit cards at the same time.

EXERCISE
UNDERSTANDING THE UTILIZATION RATIO

The utilization ratio sounds complicated at first, so we're going to break down exactly how it works. One trick is to remember 30/30. It counts for 30 percent of your credit score and you don't want to use more than 30 percent of your available credit limit.

Here's a not-so-secret truth: Credit card companies are hoping you'll end up in debt.

When a credit card lender extends you a line of credit, there is the hope that you'll buy far more than you can afford; then you'll make only the minimum-due payment, causing you to rack up interest. This is why you're lured in with sign-on bonuses of a $100 statement credit for $2,000 of spending in the first two months or 30,000 miles for $3,000 of purchases in the first three months. It's also why you're given a credit limit of $4,000 a month, even though you earn only $45,000 a year.

But credit-scoring models are eyeballing how much you use your credit card to determine if you're indulging in some risky behavior. If you keep maxing out your credit card—even if you pay it off in full—that looks risky. ("Maxing out" means using all the available credit limit.)

Using 30 percent or less of your credit limit shows restraint and responsibility. Staying in the single digits makes the credit bureaus and scoring models weak at the knees.

Here's an example:

Utilization can be calculated as the percentage you use of your total available credit limit and per individual card. Leslie has three credit cards with the following limits: $3,000, $5,000, and $2,000. She spends $1,500 a month on just one card. Leslie is 15 percent utilized because she used $1,500 of her total $10,000 credit available. However, it still doesn't look good to max out one card, even if it means using less than 30 percent of total available credit across all your cards. If Leslie is going to put $1,500 on just one card, then it should be the one with the $5,000 credit limit. 30% of $5,000 = $1,500.

Now you practice with some actual numbers!

Utilization formula

$$\frac{\text{(Total credit card balances owed)}}{\text{(Sum of available credit card limits)}} \times 100 = \text{Ratio}$$

Ron has three credit cards.

CREDIT CARD COMPANY	AVAILABLE CREDIT LIMIT	CURRENT BALANCE ON CREDIT CARD
Town Bank	$5,000	$2,100
Explorer	$7,000	$1,700
Fetch	$8,500	$3,000
TOTAL	**$20,500**	**$6,800**

What is Ron's total utilization ratio? _____ %

Here's some help:

$$\frac{\text{(Current balances owed)}}{\text{(Available credit limit)}} = \underline{\hspace{1cm}} \times 100 = \underline{\hspace{1cm}}\%$$

What about his utilization per card?

Town Bank _____ %

Explorer _____ %

Fetch _____ %

Ron's total utilization ratio is 33.17%

$$\frac{(\$6,800)}{(\$20,500)} = 0.3317 \times 100 = 33.17\%$$

Per card:

Town Bank: 42%, Explorer: 24.28%, Fetch: 35.29 %

Ron needs to lower his utilization ratio! His total utilization ratio is above 30%, which will drag down his credit score, and his utilization ratio on his Town Bank and Fetch cards are also high.

What is the maximum Ron should spend per month on each card?

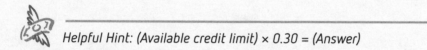

Helpful Hint: (Available credit limit) × 0.30 = (Answer)

CREDIT CARD COMPANY	AVAILABLE CREDIT LIMIT	30% OF AVAILABLE LIMIT
Town Bank	$5,000	
Explorer	$7,000	
Fetch	$8,500	

Now try this exercise with your own credit cards.

CREDIT CARD COMPANY	AVAILABLE CREDIT LIMIT	30% OF AVAILABLE CREDIT LIMIT	WHAT PERCENT I USED LAST MONTH
	$	$	%
	$	$	%
	$	$	%
	$	$	%
	$	$	%

DEBUNKING A HORRIBLE MYTH

While I have your attention in this utilization ratio section, I need to debunk a truly terrible myth.

At some point in your money journey, you may hear someone advise that you should carry a balance on your credit card from month to month.

No!

This is my pet peeve about credit scores. **You absolutely, 100 percent, unequivocally do not need to carry a balance on your credit card to build and maintain a strong credit score.**

I believe this myth comes from a misunderstanding between *having* a balance and *carrying* a balance.

If you make a purchase on your credit card but pay it off before the end of the billing cycle, then your credit card bill will probably say you have a $0 balance and owe $0. Even though you actually used your credit card, the credit bureaus often just see the report that you used $0. This might sound like you're super responsible, but in reality the credit bureau might think, "Well, if they aren't using their credit card at all, then we have no proof whether or not they can use it responsibly." This is why *having* a balance is important, but no, you don't want to *carry* a balance.

Let's use an example. I go to my favorite local bookstore to buy three books. They cost $60, and I pay with my credit card. When I receive my credit card bill, it will say my balance is $60 and my minimum due is $25.

This is *having* a balance. I will pay the full $60 bill when it's due, which means I have no credit card debt and will pay no interest.

However, if I just pay the minimum due of $25, that means $35 remains and rolls over to next month. This is *carrying* a balance (aka having credit card debt). I will now have to pay interest on the $35 I didn't pay off.

What you want is for your credit card statement (the bill) to show at least one small charge, and then as soon as the bill comes in, you pay it off on time and in full. This way you're proving that yes, you can handle using the credit card but you're not paying any interest to the bank.

BUILDING (OR REBUILDING) YOUR CREDIT SCORE

You understand how a credit score is determined and why your credit report is separate, which is an incredibly important piece of the credit history puzzle. Now let's figure out how you can build—or rebuild—a strong credit score.

The Quickest Way to Get Results (No, This Isn't a Diet Ad, I Promise)

It isn't shameful to admit you love knowing the life hack to credit success. It's why you always click on those articles like "10 Habits of the World's Richest People" or "5 Tricks to Make You Her Best Lover." Well, consider this the "3-Step Process to a Mind-Blowing Credit Score."

1. Make one or two small purchases on your credit card each month to keep your utilization ratio low (extra gold stars if you keep it below 10 percent). Sure, you can make more purchases if you want, but one or two small ones are enough to ensure that you use your credit but don't overspend.

2. Pay off all of your bills on time and in full.

3. Rinse and repeat.

Helpful Hint: Trying to make progress quickly? Consider using your credit card to autopay a small bill like a streaming service and then have your credit card bill set up to automatic payments. You can even put the credit card in a drawer somewhere. That keeps utilization low and takes the temptation to overspend out of your wallet.

This method is specific to credit cards. Factoring in student loans, auto loans, or any other installment debt you may have is equally simple: make your monthly payment on time.

Combine your monthly installment payment with the responsible use of a credit card and no lender will be able to resist you! However, you need to be able to resist your lenders. Continuing to take out loans or spending more when your credit limit is increased is how consumer debt creeps up.

EXERCISE
CREATE YOUR OWN GET-QUICK-RESULTS STRATEGY

Step 1: Look back at your utilization ratio exercise and write down how much is the maximum 30% utilization ratio for each credit card you own. Then write down the monthly due date for when you need to pay your bill.

CREDIT CARD COMPANY	30% UTILIZATION RATIO	MONTHLY DUE DATE
	$	
	$	
	$	
	$	
	$	

Step 2: Go get a piece of paper and some tape. Write the maximum you should spend on that card in the month and the credit card bill due date on a strip of paper and tape it to your credit card.

Step 3: Write down a realistic plan for how you can use your credit card for one or two small purchases each month.

I would normally buy _____, *which costs* $_____, *and*

_____, *which costs* $_____.

or

I pay for _____ *service monthly, which costs* $_____. *I can auto-mate that payment and pay my credit card bill on time and in full on* _____/_____/20___.

Step 4: Write down all your loans, the monthly payments, and the due dates. Add these due dates to your calendar or preferred reminder method to ensure you never miss a payment!

LOAN NAME	MONTHLY PAYMENT	DUE DATE
	$	
	$	
	$	
	$	
	$	
	$	
	$	

Have you considered automating your loan payments? It can ensure you never miss a payment as long as you always have enough money in the account. However, it's good to double-check that the payment actually went through each month. Systems can fail, so you don't want to end up being in default because you just didn't notice the autopay system malfunctioned.

I KEEP GETTING REJECTED FOR A CREDIT CARD. WHAT SHOULD I DO?

You need strong credit history to get approved for a credit card, but a credit card helps you build said stellar credit history. It's the financial world's mind-boggling version of the chicken-or-the-egg scenario. But don't worry. You won't need to get all Philosophy 101 with a credit card application in order to get approved for a card.

Get a Secured Card

Credit card companies offer a beginner-level credit card known as a secured card.

You'll need to plop down a deposit in order to open one. The amount required varies based on the credit card company, but it'll usually range from $50 to $200. The deposit typically serves as your credit limit and is refundable *if* your card is in good standing when you close it down. Failure to pay your bills means relinquishing your deposit and doing absolutely nothing to build your credit history. #DoubleFail.

Be sure to research a secured card before you apply. You shouldn't be paying activation fees or annual fees for a secured card.

Helpful Hint: Mitigate the risk of rejection by seeing if you're preapproved for a credit card. Many of the major credit card companies offer the option to check if you're prequalified (or preapproved) online. Just Google the name of a credit card company you're interested in and "prequalified" to find these landing pages. You'll need to input your name, address, and the last four digits of your Social Security number. Being prequalified doesn't guarantee you'll get the card, but it reduces the risk of rejection. It also won't harm your credit score to check for preapproval.

How to Properly Utilize a Secured Card for Quickest Results

1. Put down your deposit and make sure you know your credit limit. In this example, it's going to be $200.

2. Use your secured card to make one small purchase each month. You can even keep the card out of your wallet entirely and just set it up to pay a small recurring monthly bill like your preferred streaming service.

3. Never use more than 30% of your limit, so no more than $60 of a $200 limit.

4. Pay off the card on time and in full each month.

5. Monitor your credit score by using one of the many free tools available like: Credit Karma, Capital One's CreditWise, American Express's MyCredit Guide, Mint, or Credit Sesame.

6. Once your credit score creeps above 680 or you suddenly find that you're starting to get prequalified letters in the mail, then apply for a regular unsecured credit card. Just be sure to properly vet the card because you may get some crappy offers early on. It should be a card with no annual fee and no activation fee.

7. Wait until you've been approved and received your new no-training-wheels-needed credit card before calling to close down your secured card and getting your deposit back.

THAT'S A LOT of information about credit scores and credit reports! But to be honest, it's just a taste compared to the chapter in *Broke Millennial: Stop Scraping By and Get Your Financial Life Together.* If this isn't quite enough and you want an even deeper dive about understanding, building, and protecting your credit report and score, then check out chapter 6 in *Broke Millennial.*

Before you move on to learning more about how to use credit cards—you need to pass this pop quiz!

EXERCISE
POP QUIZ: CREDIT MYTH BUSTER

There are soooo many myths out there when it comes to building and maintaining a strong credit score and report. Let's see how well you can bust them in this true or false quiz. You can find the answers in the back of the book on page 271.

Circle whether the answer is true or false.

1. Checking my credit report will hurt my score.

    True/False

2. A potential employer can check my credit score.

    True/False

3. I should carry a balance month to month on my credit card.

    True/False

4. It's good to max out my credit card or get close to the limit.

    True/False

5. It's better to just use a prepaid card or debit card instead of a credit card.

    True/False

6. Don't accept a credit limit increase from your credit card company.

    True/False

7. Never close your oldest credit card.

    True/False

KEY TAKEAWAYS FOR UNDERSTANDING, BUILDING, AND MAINTAINING A HEALTHY CREDIT HISTORY

→ There are three credit bureaus: Equifax, TransUnion, and Experian.

→ Your goal is to be in the 700+ credit score club.

→ Always pay your credit card off on time and in full.

→ Lenders aren't required to report your information to all three bureaus.

→ Routinely monitoring your credit score is a simple way to detect identity theft.

→ Pulling your own credit report doesn't harm your credit score.

→ A soft pull lets a lender get a peek at your report without harming your credit score, while a hard pull leaves an inquiry on your credit report and results in a small dip in your credit score.

→ Shopping around for the best rate on a mortgage, auto loan, or personal loan will result in just one hard inquiry on your credit report if you do it within a 14-day window. The credit bureaus understand you're just looking for the best deal.

→ Don't stress so much about hard inquiries on your credit report. Your credit score isn't a trophy; it's meant to be used to get you better financial products.

GET YOUR FINANCIAL LIFE TOGETHER CHECK-IN

What is your biggest takeaway (or aha moment) from this chapter?

_____.

_____.

_____.

What feels the most overwhelming about this chapter?

_____.

_____.

_____.

Why does it feel so overwhelming to you in this moment?

_____.

_____.

_____.

Based on what you just learned, write down one actionable step you can take this week to improve your financial life.

_____.

_____.

_____.

Chapter 7

Wait, *This* Is How I'm Supposed to Use My Credit Cards?!

CREDIT CARDS ARE a powerful tool, when used correctly.

Here's the credit card résumé:

- Credit cards can help you build and maintain a healthy credit score.

- Credit cards provide better identity theft security than their debit card counterparts, because compromised cards don't provide direct access to your bank account.

- Credit cards offer rewards that can be leveraged for cash back, free flights, hotel stays, airline elite member status, and a whole lot more.

- Credit cards can provide insurance when making purchases (e.g., being able to dispute a payment if an item you bought never arrived or was damaged) or even insurance when you travel (e.g., money to cover meals and lodging if your flight gets canceled or delayed overnight).

There are a lot of advantages to using a credit card, but those advantages only exist if you avoid credit card debt.

Disclaimer: This chapter takes the firm stance that you should use a credit card only if you can afford to pay it off on time and in full. This, as a general policy, is how I feel about credit cards. However, there are times when life can hit hard and a credit card gets used as a backup emergency fund (or a primary emergency fund). That reality is not being dismissed by the language in this chapter. A global pandemic certainly taught us that you can do absolutely everything correctly and still end up needing to rely on credit cards through no fault of your own. I push the pay-in-full rhetoric so hard because the goal is to avoid credit card debt, and it's also easy to get confused by the language on credit card statements if you're new to using them.

HOW A CREDIT CARD COMPANY MAKES MONEY

In theory, a credit card offers access to a monthly loan. The credit card company gives you a piece of plastic that allows you to make purchases up to a predetermined limit. You then make the purchases you want and have the option to either:

1. Pay the entire bill when your statement comes in

2. Just pay the minimum due

3. Pay more than the minimum due, aka pay the minimum plus an additional amount, but not the entire bill

For example, you spent $500 on your credit card this month. You've received your bill and it says:

Statement balance: $500

Minimum amount due: $25

You can pay one of these three options:

1. $500

2. $25

3. $25 + (whatever else you can afford)

It will be an on-time payment so long as you pay at least the minimum due by the bill's due date. **But paying anything less than the statement balance means you're now carrying credit card debt.**

It's really easy to get confused the first time you open up a credit card bill. Right there in bold it says **minimum due**. Sometimes this is the first line item on your bill, even above the total due. **It's almost as if the minimum payment due is what you're *supposed* to pay. It's not. It's what the credit card company wants you to pay.** You're supposed to (and should) pay the full balance due.

A credit card company makes money only when you trip up and pay less than the full balance due. How? Because you'll owe interest on the amount you don't pay back.

If there's only one major takeaway from this section, it's this . . . the first rule of using a credit card: *Pay it off on time and in full.* Never carry a balance month to month. The right way to use a credit is simple: *Don't charge more than you can afford to pay off every single month. Then pay it off!*

EXERCISE
READING THAT CREDIT CARD BILL

Go download a recent credit card statement.

Helpful Hint: Log in to your account and just CTRL-F for "statement" if you're not sure where to find one.

Fill in the information below based on your most recent statement.

Statement balance: $_____
   (Sometimes called New Balance or Current Balance)

Minimum payment due: $_____

Fees: $_____

Interest: $_____

APR (Annual Percentage Rate aka interest charged): _____%

Late payment costs are $_____ *and penalty APR is* _____%.

💡 _____

Did You Know: A late payment will not only cost you a fee and switch your interest rate to the penalty APR, but it can have a huge impact on your credit score.
_____

Now that you're more familiar with the credit card statement, we're going to bring back some elements of chapter 5 and properly analyze your credit cards. It's important to assess your financial products at least once a year and make sure they're still the right fit for you.

EXERCISE
HI, CREDIT CARD. NICE TO MEET YOU

Fill out the grid on the next page. Most of this information can be found on your credit card statement, but some might also require you to do a little research online. Googling your credit card name plus "benefits" will usually get you to the necessary landing pages.

Annual Fee: Are you being charged a fee for this card?

Interest Rate: How much is the bank charging you if you carry a balance? This is written as APR (annual percentage rate).

Penalty APR: How much will your interest rate increase and what fees will you need to pay if you miss a monthly payment?

Types of Rewards: Does your credit card offer you rewards like flat-rate cash back on everything or increased cash back in certain categories or cash back on rotating categories?

Other Benefits: Besides the reward structure, are there other benefits from this credit card? For example, a sign-on bonus, rebates, access to certain clubs, or travel insurance.

CREDIT CARD COMPANY	ANNUAL FEE	INTEREST RATE (APR)	PENALTY APR + FEES	TYPE OF REWARDS	OTHER BENEFITS
	$	%			
	$	%			
	$	%			
	$	%			
	$	%			
	$	%			

EXERCISE
CREDIT CARD ANALYSIS

You've collected the information. Now it's time to see if these credit cards are actually working for you. This is especially important if you've signed up for credit cards to chase a sign-on bonus, which is common with travel hackers. Are all of your cards still serving you, or is the annual fee now a waste of money?

The credit cards I use most are:

_____.

_____.

They serve me well because:

_____.

Do the rewards or other perks you get from your credit cards truly offset the cost of the annual fee? If yes, explain why for each card with an annual fee.

_____.

_____.

_____.

_____.

Am I receiving the same benefits from multiple credit cards with annual fees?

_____.

_____.

_____.

Am I currently using these benefits across all of my cards with a high fee?

_____.

Is there another, cheaper way to receive these same perks?

_____.

_____.

_____.

_____.

These credit cards are the ones I should keep:

_____.

_____.

These credit cards are no longer serving me, and I should close them:

_____.

_____.

Did You Know: Yes, closing down a credit card can (and probably will) impact your credit score. This is particularly true if it's your oldest card. It's often a good strategy to keep your oldest credit card open, even if you don't use it much. But if it has a high annual fee, you could call the credit card company and see if you can get it switched to a different, no-annual-fee card with that bank (often called downgrading). The dip in your score will be temporary as long as you have other positive behaviors— like paying your bills on time and low utilization! It's usually not a big deal unless you're planning to apply for a mortgage or another big loan in the coming months.

TELL ME MORE ABOUT CREDIT CARD REWARDS

Rewards have been mentioned a few times at this point. If you're new to credit cards (or you've never had one), it's possible you aren't too familiar with the reward possibilities out there. I've paid for flights and hotels entirely from credit card rewards, which is a massive benefit, but it's also easy to trip up!

Go slowly upon entering the credit card rewards game. You need to first figure out the "why" for the rewards. Is this credit card for basic cash back on every purchase, or are you looking to book a free flight? Starting in the cash back arena to warm up is usually the better option for a rookie.

There are three main types of cash back reward cards on the market today:

1. Flat-rate cash back

2. Rotating categories

3. Sign-on bonus

Flat-rate cash back cards mean you get a percentage back on every single purchase, usually 1.5% to 2%.

Rotating categories offer a spiked percentage in a niche category for a quarter of the year, such as 5% cash back on restaurants and movies from January to March and then 5% back on gas from April to June and so on. Then all other purchases usually earn around 1%. The categories often have some sort of opt-in option, so if you forget to sign up for the rotating 5% cash back, then you'll just be earning 1%.

Sign-on bonus offers a big onetime reward if you spend a certain amount in a set period of time. A common example would be 50,000 frequent flyer miles if you spend $3,000 within three months of opening the card. These cards usually have an annual fee. Sometimes the annual fee is still worth paying because the bonus is so high or because other benefits included in the card offset the fee's cost, even with a high annual fee.

For example, a card might have a $500 annual fee, but offers a $300 travel rebate and covers the cost of a Global Entry application ($100) and gets you lounge access at airports. Even without figuring out the cost of lounge access, that's $400 back on a $500 fee—so the remaining $100 spent might be worth it to some people.

EXERCISE
AM I READY FOR A REWARDS CARD?

Take the quiz below by circling True or False.

1. You haven't had credit card debt for at least two years.

   True/False

2. You've never missed making a payment on a loan or credit card.

   True/False

3. A sign-on bonus required spend is within your regular monthly budget and you wouldn't be overspending just to get a reward.

   True/False

4. You've never struggled with compulsive shopping or buying.

   True/False

5. You have the foundation of your financial life laid, including an emergency savings fund.

   True/False

If you answered False to any of these questions, then it's probably not a financially wise decision for you to chase after credit card rewards.

It is really tempting to chase credit card rewards, but it's not something everyone should do! Be brutally honest with yourself. Ending up in credit card debt isn't worth bonus miles or cash.

BE IN THE KNOW! SET UP ALERTS

Fraud is an unfortunate reality and you—yes, you reading this book—will experience some form of identity theft. One of the most common is credit card or debit card fraud. Thieves can get access to your information in a variety of ways including skimmers on card readers and data breaches or by simply stealing your wallet.

Credit cards come with excellent fraud protection, especially if you report the fraud early. You generally will not be liable for the charges made—but it is important you report quickly, which is why I highly recommend you set up alerts.

Most credit card providers give you the option to set up alerts about your credit card activity via e-mail or text message or both if you really want to be informed. The reason for setting up alerts for your credit card activity is twofold:

1. You get bugged with each transaction and get daily or weekly reminders of your overall balance, so there's no way to get punched in the mouth by your credit card bill at the end of the month.

2. You immediately know when someone is trying to scam your card for a huge shopping spree—or in two of my own experiences, a sub from Jersey Mike's in Georgia (I live in New York) or $70 on McDonald's via Grubhub.

Credit card companies usually make it quite simple to set up alerts and don't charge for the service. They're all quick to remind you to check and see if your cell phone carrier charges for texts (because it's still the early 2000s apparently).

Setting up text alerts is a free and easy way to monitor your spending habits and the security of your credit card. You can set this up on the credit card's site, usually under "Profile & Settings" and then "alerts." You should set the minimum threshold as $0.01 because some scammers will try making a super-small purchase just to see if the card works and not to draw attention at first.

P.S. You can also set up alerts for transactions on your checking and savings accounts, and I recommend you set those alerts up too, especially if you frequently use a debit card to make purchases.

IS "BUY NOW, PAY LATER" THE SAME AS A CREDIT CARD?

Buy Now, Pay Later (BNPL) is an additional way to make installment payments on a purchase. No, it's not the same as a credit card. It's almost as if a personal loan and a credit card had a baby. BNPL services (like Affirm, Klarna, Afterpay) are usually presented as an option when you're ready to check out online or in stores.

Not all BNPL services operate in the same way, but you usually put a little bit down and then the rest of your bill is split up into four installments over the coming months. These installment payments can be interest-free so long as you pay on time, but some consumers will be required to pay interest depending on credit worthiness. While it might not hurt your credit to sign up for a service, it will crush your credit if you miss payments. At the time of this writing, most BNPL programs do not help boost your credit either because they don't report their short-term installment loans to credit bureaus unless you miss a payment.

BNPL is an emerging market that is likely to see changes over time, so be sure to do your own research before using one.

"USING A CREDIT CARD" CHECKLIST

→ Charge only what you can afford to pay off each month.

→ Pay your card on time, on the due date listed on the statement.

→ Pay the amount due in full every month.

→ *If* you find one month that you need to charge more than you can afford to pay off, then always pay as much above the minimum balance due as possible.

→ Set up account alerts to notify you of your balance and when a transaction occurs.

→ Rewards should complement your spending habits; don't change your spending to earn rewards.

- -

GET YOUR FINANCIAL LIFE TOGETHER CHECK-IN

What is your biggest takeaway (or aha moment) from this chapter?

_____.

_____.

_____.

What feels most overwhelming about this chapter?

_____.

_____.

_____.

Why does it feel so overwhelming to you in this moment?

_____.

_____.

_____.

Based on what you just learned, write down one actionable step you can take this week to improve your financial life.

_____.

_____.

_____.

Chapter 8

Yikes, I Have Debt. What Now?

How COMFORTABLE ARE you talking about your debt? Do your friends or partner know you have debt? Do they know how much or what types?

It's okay if your answers are "Not at all comfortable," "No, they don't," and "Absolutely not."

Debt is a complicated topic because of how much control we allow it to have over our lives.

We feel guilt for creating and/or carrying debt.

We feel stress trying to manage our debt.

We feel shame when admitting to its existence.

WHICH TYPE(S) OF DEBT DO YOU HAVE?

Circle all the ones that apply to you.

AUTO LOAN	MORTGAGE
CREDIT CARD	OWE A FRIEND/FAMILY MEMBER
FEDERAL AND/OR PRIVATE STUDENT LOANS	PAYDAY OR TITLE LOANS
	PERSONAL LOANS
MEDICAL BILLS	

EXERCISE
RANT IT OUT

I know it doesn't feel good to confront your debt, but it's part of the process of taking financial control. Before we dig in further, let's touch base with your emotions.

How does each one of your debts make you feel?

_____.

_____.

_____.

_____.

What physical sensations do you experience when you allow yourself to think about your debt?

_____.

_____.

_____.

_____.

Why do you think your debt makes you feel this way?

_____.

_____.

_____.

_____.

What makes you angriest or most resentful about your debt?

_____.

_____.

_____.

_____.

There's a really big secret I want to share with you:

You don't need to assign morality to your debt.

Debt is the dirtiest four-letter in personal finance, but only because there are people who assign morality to debt. It's okay for your debts to create emotional reactions in you because there are different circumstances under which you ended up owing a lender money. This isn't to dismiss your feelings, *but* the truth is, it's harmful to think of debt as good or bad. Oftentimes you hear about "good debt" like a mortgage or student loans because it helped you acquire an asset or get an education. Then there's "bad debt" like credit cards because it's supposedly saying something about your character or ability to handle your finances.

Frankly, debt is just debt. It's a tool that gets used when you don't have enough money to make a purchase up front. At times, that can be really advantageous and an investment that pays off. Other times, it's not. We don't need to assign guilt or morality to debt because it isn't helpful. The shame spiral is not a motivational way to get your financial life together. Instead, take a deep breath and dramatically exhale (or even scream if it won't startle anyone!) your toxic feelings about your debt.

Do you feel at least a little lighter?

You're going to feel a whole lot lighter after we work through creating a plan for you to tackle your debt. Just because I said you shouldn't assign morality to your debt doesn't mean you get a pass to dismiss it or keep accumulating more of it.

This process will require diligence, patience, fortitude, and pretty much every other motivational platitude you've seen on a poster in the hallways of your office. Basically, it will require you to battle your frustrations and occasional impulses to spend, track your spending patterns, negotiate or pick up another stream of income, or even alter your lifestyle for a period of time.

TIME TO ASSESS THE SITUATION

It's impossible to make a plan without first understanding where you stand. Facing the reality of your total debt picture can be stressful, intimidating, and demoralizing. Instead, just accept it for what it is: the situation. Old You made some decisions (or was forced into making tough choices) and Current You is dealing with the debt as a result. Forgive your past self and don't dwell on those choices. It's a waste of your energy. Now you focus on making a plan and putting in the work to get debt-free.

EXERCISE
FACE YOUR NUMBERS.

Helpful Hint: You probably already have this information from chapter 3 when you calculated your DTI. But the details might've changed since then, so it never hurts to update!

TYPE OF DEBT	LENDER	MINIMUM DUE	TOTAL AMOUNT OWED	APR (INTEREST RATE)
		$	$	%
		$	$	%
		$	$	%
		$	$	%
		$	$	%
		$	$	%
		$	$	%
		$	$	%
		$	$	%

TOTAL $_____   TOTAL $_____

HOLD UP, SHOULD I BE TREATING ALL MY DEBT THE SAME?

Excellent question. No, you shouldn't. While we don't want to assign morality to debt, we must acknowledge the reality that all debt isn't created equal. Consumer debt like credit cards, medical, payday, or even an auto loan should be prioritized over a mortgage or federal student loans.

There are a few reasons.

1. Credit cards usually have the highest interest rates (next to payday and title loans), so you usually want to knock those out the fastest.

2. Your mortgage doesn't necessarily need to be paid off quickly. Sure, it's probably lovely to own your home outright, but you might want to be focusing on other financial goals besides paying off your home, especially if it has a low interest rate. It can even make sense to focus on prioritizing investing over paying off your mortgage quickly.

3. Student loans have lower interest rates than credit cards, so it makes sense for student loans to be the second-tier focus on your debt payoff journey if you have credit card debt. Plus, the potential for student loan forgiveness and other perks for federal loans makes it less compelling to aggressively pay those off in lieu of having money for other financial goals. This, however, does not apply to private student loans. Private student loans do not have the same benefits as federal student loans and often have higher interest rates. We'll get into the nuances of student loans in the next chapter.

Critical Knowledge: No matter which debt repayment strategy you pick, there's one key truth. Paying more than the minimum due is what helps you get to your debt-free deadline. Even just a little bit above the minimum due helps!

CREATE AN EFFECTIVE DEBT REPAYMENT PLAN

There are many ways to create a debt repayment plan, but two of the most effective are Debt Snowball and Debt Avalanche.

Debt Snowball focuses on the psychology of giving you a quick success to encourage you to keep trucking along.

Debt Avalanche focuses on the math and aims to ensure you pay the least amount in interest.

As you read more about these techniques, please keep in mind that personal finance is nothing if not *personal*. The rational part of your brain may scream at you to go the mathematical route to pay less interest, but if you're someone who needs to see quick results (which, let's admit, is the majority of us), then the mental boost method may be the one that actually keeps you on track.

Debt Avalanche

The Debt Avalanche is often referred to as the "right way" to pay down your debt. **It is the option that leaves the most money safely in your bank account instead of in the hands of your lenders.** However, it could also be the option that's most likely to lead you back to your life of overspending. You may feel like it's taking forever to make any progress on your debt repayment, so what's the point?

Here's how it works.

Step 1:   Write a list of your debts, arranging them from *highest interest rate to lowest interest rate*.

Helpful Hint: You should have all this from the Face Your Numbers exercise, but if you struggled to find information about the APR on your cards on your monthly statement, now's the time to find it out.

TYPE OF DEBT	LENDER	APR (INTEREST RATE)	TOTAL AMOUNT OWED	MINIMUM DUE
		%	$	$
		%	$	$
		%	$	$
		%	$	$
		%	$	$
		%	$	$
		%	$	$
		%	$	$
		%	$	$

For example, Pete and his wife, Paula, have the following debts:

TYPE OF DEBT	LENDER	APR (INTEREST RATE)	TOTAL AMOUNT OWED	MINIMUM DUE
Credit card	Town Bank	24.99%	$3,000	$90
Credit card	Orange Store	22.99%	$700	$25
Auto loan	Friendly Bank	5.5%	$1,200	$36
Student loan	Great Ponds	4.5%	$10,000	$103

Step 2: Evaluate how much you have to put toward all your debts each month. Refer back to the cash flow you created in chapter 4 and see what you can free up each month to focus on your debt repayment plan. Another option is to evaluate how you can earn more and use the additional income to go toward debt payoff.

I have $_____ per month I can put toward my debt payoff plan.

Step 3: Any extra dollars go toward the debt with the *highest interest rate.*

⚠️ *Pay the minimums across all your other balances. You should not stop making the minimum payments on your other debts during this process.*

TYPE OF DEBT	LENDER	APR (INTEREST RATE)	TOTAL AMOUNT OWED	MINIMUM DUE	MONTHLY PAYMENT YOU CAN MAKE
		%	$	$	$
The extra money only gets added to the debt at the top of your list					
		%	$	$	$
		%	$	$	$
		%	$	$	$
		%	$	$	$
		%	$	$	$
		%	$	$	$
		%	$	$	$
		%	$	$	$

For example, Pete and Paula owe $254 a month at minimum, but they've run the numbers and determined they can afford to put $330 toward their debt each month. That means $76 can get added to the minimum due of the debt with the highest interest rate, their Town Bank credit card. Pete and Paula continue to pay the minimums due on the rest of their debts.

TYPE OF DEBT	LENDER	APR (INTEREST RATE)	TOTAL AMOUNT OWED	MINIMUM DUE	MONTHLY PAYMENT PETE & PAULA CAN MAKE
Credit card	Town Bank	24.99%	$3,000	$90	$166
Credit card	Orange Store	22.99%	$700	$25	$25
Auto loan	Friendly Bank	5.5%	$1,200	$36	$36
Student loan	Great Ponds	4.5%	$10,000	$103	$103

Step 4: When debt at the top of the list gets knocked out, you then combine that monthly payment with the next minimum payment due.

Let's look at Pete and Paula's example. They paid off the Town Bank credit card. The $166 payment that was going to Town Bank now gets added to the $25 monthly payment to the Orange Store credit card for $191 per month.

(For the sake of simplicity, we'll say that Pete and Paula's other debts stayed at the same amounts despite making the monthly minimum payment due.)

TYPE OF DEBT	LENDER	APR (INTEREST RATE)	TOTAL AMOUNT OWED	MINIMUM DUE	MONTHLY PAYMENT PETE & PAULA CAN MAKE
Credit card	Orange Store	22.99%	$700	$25	$191
Auto loan	Friendly Bank	5.5%	$1,200	$36	$36
Student loan	Great Ponds	4.5%	$10,000	$103	$103

What will happen with your debt in Debt Avalanche?

Once I pay off my _____ debt, the $_____ monthly payment I was

making now gets added to my _____ debt. I'll then be paying $_____

per month toward that debt.

This process keeps repeating until all that money is focused on your final debt with the lowest interest rate.

Here's how Pete and Paula's plays out.

TYPE OF DEBT	LENDER	APR (INTEREST RATE)	TOTAL AMOUNT OWED	MINIMUM DUE	MONTHLY PAYMENT PETE & PAULA CAN MAKE
Auto loan	Friendly Bank	5.5%	$1,200	$36	$227
Student loan	Great Ponds	4.5%	$10,000	$103	$103

TYPE OF DEBT	LENDER	APR (INTEREST RATE)	TOTAL AMOUNT OWED	MINIMUM DUE	MONTHLY PAYMENT PETE & PAULA CAN MAKE
Student loan	Great Ponds	4.5%	$10,000	$103	$330

It will take Pete and Paula 51 months (a little over four years) and cost about $2,500 in interest to get debt-free using Debt Avalanche. If Pete and Paula had just paid the minimums due, it would have taken them nearly 10 years to be debt-free and cost more than $5,000 in interest alone. Any additional money Pete and Paula could've put toward their debt would've brought down the timeline even more. For example, increasing by $20 to $350 a month would've reduced the timeline to 48 months and meant only $2,260 in interest.

Want to play around with your own Debt Avalanche plan? I recommend the free tool Undebt.it by going to undebt.it/debt-avalanche-calculator.php.*

Debt Snowball

The Debt Snowball method focuses more on the psychology of doing something difficult. Debt repayment can feel like a never-ending slog with a finish line that seems to keep creeping farther away no matter how hard you try. **The Debt Snowball strategy is designed to give you faster, incremental wins to help keep you motivated on the journey.**

Instead of focusing on knocking out those higher interest rate debts first, you're not going to even pay attention to interest. You're going to rank your debts from the lowest balance to the highest balance.

The Debt Snowball strategy does have you end up paying more in interest, *but* it could keep you on target to actually pay off the debt in the first place. If you'll respond better to this method, it'll actually save you money, because at least the debt will eventually get paid off entirely.

Debt Snowball and Debt Avalanche are similar in almost every other way except for how you're prioritizing the debts to pay off.

> **Step 1:** Write a list of your debts, arranging them from *the lowest balance to the highest balance.*

Let's return to our friends Pete and Paula. This time their debts are ordered as:

TYPE OF DEBT	LENDER	TOTAL AMOUNT OWED	MINIMUM DUE
Credit card	Orange Store	$700	$25
Auto loan	Friendly Bank	$1,200	$36
Credit card	Town Bank	$3,000	$90
Student loan	Great Ponds	$10,000	$103

---

* At the time of this writing in 2022, Undebt.it is a free online resource. I have never received compensation nor collaborated with Undebt.it and have no financial investment in the company.

Step 2: Evaluate how much you have to put toward all your debts each month.

I have $_____ per month I can put toward my debt payoff plan.

Step 3: Any extra dollars go toward the debt with the *lowest balance*.

⚠ *Pay the minimums across all your other balances. You should not stop making the minimum payments on your other debts during this process.*

TYPE OF DEBT	LENDER	TOTAL AMOUNT OWED	MINIMUM DUE	MONTHLY PAYMENT YOU CAN MAKE
		$	$	$
The extra money only gets added to the debt at the top of your list				
		$	$	$
		$	$	$
		$	$	$
		$	$	$
		$	$	$
		$	$	$
		$	$	$
		$	$	$

We know Pete and Paula owe $254 a month at minimum, but can afford to put $330 toward their debt each month. This time, the extra $76 goes toward the Orange Store credit card first because it has the lowest balance.

TYPE OF DEBT	LENDER	TOTAL AMOUNT OWED	MINIMUM DUE	MONTHLY PAYMENT PETE & PAULA CAN MAKE
Credit card	Orange Store	$700	$25	$101
Auto loan	Friendly Bank	$1,200	$36	$36
Credit card	Town Bank	$3,000	$90	$90
Student loan	Great Ponds	$10,000	$103	$103

Step 4: When debt at the top of the list gets knocked out, you combine that monthly payment with the next minimum payment due.

Let's look at Pete and Paula's example. They paid off the Orange Store credit card. The $101 payment that was going to Orange Store now gets added to the $36 monthly payment to the Friendly Bank auto loan for $137 per month.

(For the sake of simplicity, we'll say that Pete and Paula's other debts stayed at the same amounts despite making the monthly minimum payment due.)

TYPE OF DEBT	LENDER	TOTAL AMOUNT OWED	MINIMUM DUE	MONTHLY PAYMENT PETE & PAULA CAN MAKE
Auto loan	Friendly Bank	$1,200	$36	$137
Credit card	Town Bank	$3,000	$90	$90
Student loan	Great Ponds	$10,000	$103	$103

What will happen with your debt using the Debt Snowball strategy?

Once I pay off my _____ debt, the $_____ monthly payment I was

making now gets added to my _____ debt. I'll then be paying $_____

per month toward that debt.

This process keeps repeating until all that money is focused on your final debt with the highest balance.

Here's how Pete and Paula's plays out.

TYPE OF DEBT	LENDER	TOTAL AMOUNT OWED	MINIMUM DUE	MONTHLY PAYMENT PETE & PAULA CAN MAKE
Credit card	Town Bank	$3,000	$90	$227
Student loan	Great Ponds	$10,000	$103	$103

TYPE OF DEBT	LENDER	TOTAL AMOUNT OWED	MINIMUM DUE	MONTHLY PAYMENT PETE & PAULA CAN MAKE
Student loan	Great Ponds	$10,000	$103	$330

It will take Pete and Paula 52 months and cost about $2,700 in interest to get debt-free using Debt Snowball. That's one month longer and a little over $200 extra in interest compared to Debt Avalanche.

If Pete and Paula had just paid the minimums due on their debts, it still would've taken them nearly 10 years to be debt-free and cost more than $5,000 in interest alone.

Want to play around with your own Debt Snowball plan? Try the Undebt.it snowball calculator: undebt.it/debt-snowball-calculator.php.

DEBT AVALANCHE OR DEBT SNOWBALL: WHICH SHOULD I USE?

People often get stuck on "which is right" when it comes to deciding between these two strategies. Here's a secret: There is no "right." It's all about what works best for you! Answer these questions honestly:

1. I'm excited about saving more money over the course of debt repayment, even if it takes longer to see progress.

   True/False

2. I definitely need to see progress quickly in order to stay motivated.

   True/False

A yes to question one means avalanche is a good fit, and a yes to question two means snowball is your preferred option.

The strategy that keeps you on track to pay off your debt is the one that's right for you! It's also okay if you decide to switch or come up with your own hybrid along the way, especially as you learn about other ways to pay off consumer debt.

OTHER WAYS TO PAY OFF CONSUMER DEBT

Balance Transfer

Do you trust yourself to open a credit card and never charge anything to it?

YES / NO

Your answer to that question, assuming you were being honest, is critical. If you just circled no, then skip this section and move on. It is 100% not worth the risk. If you said yes, let's talk about balance transfers.

A balance transfer allows you to move your outstanding credit card balance with Bank A to a new card with Bank B. Bank B will offer you something like 0 percent APR for 18 months (probably with a 3 percent fee) if you transfer your debt. This is a good idea because 0 percent

APR means you aren't getting charged interest, so every penny from your monthly payment will go toward the principal debt you owe. This discount on your APR is known as a "promotional rate" or "intro rate." It only lasts for a limited period of time before spiking to a regular APR.

Why would a bank be willing to offer you such a sweet deal? Because debt is hugely profitable to the banks, and the bank is willing to make a bet that you're going to screw up and stay in debt, thus owe them interest. In the bank's mind, you've already messed up before to get into debt in the first place, so why not again? But here's the secret: You're not going to screw up again!

Let's look at an example of how a balance transfer can save you lots of money.

Frank collects hats and ends up $4,000 in credit card debt when he overindulges in his hobby. Bank A charges him 17 percent APR a month on his $4,000 in debt. He pays $170 a month toward his card, but it feels like the debt never gets smaller. At this rate, it will take him nearly 2.5 years and cost him nearly $900 in interest to pay off his credit card. Frank uses a balance transfer offer from Bank B to move his debt to a card offering 0 percent APR for 18 months. He'll pay a 3 percent fee on that $4,000 (so $120) to move the debt, and the card will charge him 18 percent interest after the promotional period ends in month 19.

Even with the 3 percent fee, Frank pays only $180 in interest and fees and is done with paying off his debt in 25 months. That's a savings of nearly $720. Frank could even pay it off in 18 months and pay only $120 in fees if he increases his monthly payments from $170 to $230.

EXERCISE
PICKING THE RIGHT BALANCE TRANSFER CARD

1. Fill in the table below with details about your credit card debt.

BANK	APR	MONTHLY MINIMUM DUE	TOTAL BALANCE OWED
	%	$	$
	%	$	$
	%	$	$
	%	$	$
	%	$	$

Looking at this information, highlight (or star) the credit card you'd most like to pay off first. This could be based on the highest interest rate, the highest balance, or just the one that annoys you the most.

2. What is your current credit score? (Your credit card might offer you access to your credit score, or you can use options like Credit Karma, Capital One's CreditWise, or Experian's free credit score.)

   My credit score is _____.

You need a credit score of at least 680 (but 700+ is better) to have strong odds of being approved for a balance transfer credit card. That doesn't mean you'll for sure be denied if your score is under 680, but you might want to focus on increasing your credit score first before applying.

3. Ready to apply for a balance transfer? Look at the name of the bank with the highlight or star. You aren't applying for a balance transfer there. There's no real incentive for the bank that currently holds your debt to suddenly drop your rate to 0% APR. Instead, you're going to shop around among its competitors. It's best if you don't have an existing credit card with those competitors. For example, if you have credit cards with Bank A and Bank B, but you're looking for a balance transfer to pay off Bank A's debt, then it's best to apply with Bank C. Bank B still has some of your debt, so it also might not be inclined to give you a good balance transfer deal. You usually need to be a new customer for the best deal.

4. Research your balance transfer options. You might have gotten direct mail (actual mail in your mailbox) with offers or e-mails from banks promoting a balance transfer. You can also use financial product comparison sites like NerdWallet or Bankrate. Other options are to go directly to a bank's website to see the offers or to Google the bank's name and "balance transfer."

5. Aim to find a minimum of three offers. Don't apply yet; just look at the terms offered.

BANK	DO I HAVE A CREDIT CARD HERE?	PROMOTIONAL APR OFFER	LENGTH OF PROMOTIONAL RATE	FEE	COST OF FEE*
	YES / NO	%	months	%	$
	YES / NO	%	months	%	$
	YES / NO	%	months	%	$
	YES / NO	%	months	%	$
	YES / NO	%	months	%	$

* You calculate the cost of the fee as a percentage of the balance you're going to roll over. For example, you want to move a balance of $3,000. The balance transfer fee is 5%. $3,000 × 0.05 = $150. The cost of the fee is $150.

Helpful Hint: The fee for the balance transfer is usually worth it based on how much you would otherwise be paying in interest to the bank that currently owns your credit card debt. But it is always important to do the math for yourself.

6. Look at the table in step 5 and determine which balance transfer offer is the most beneficial for you. Hint: probably the one with the longest promotional term + lowest rate. Highlight the option you choose.

7. Make sure the promotional interest rate is waived. There are two types of promotional interest rates: waived and deferred. Waived means you cannot retroactively be charged interest. If you don't pay off the balance during the promotional period, then you'll owe interest only on the remaining balance. Deferred isn't so kind. Fail to pay off the total balance during the promotional period? You'll owe retroactively for all the interest that would've accrued during the promotional period. Store cards are notorious for this trap, so be wary if you're financing furniture or clothing on a card with 0% financing.

8. The promotional interest rate on my balance transfer offer is _____%.

9. Once you've fully vetted the different offers and have selected the best one for you, it's time to actually apply and see if you're approved!

10. Got rejected? It's okay. There are lots of reasons why that can happen. Your credit score might be one. Perhaps it's your DTI (remember this from chapter 3?). A high debt-to-income ratio, especially above 40%, could be cause for rejection. You could try applying for another offer at a different bank or spend time improving your score/lowering your DTI before applying again.

EXERCISE
MAKING THE MOST OF YOUR BALANCE TRANSFER CARD

Congrats, you've picked and been approved for your balance transfer credit card!

Time to make the most of the promotional period to aggressively pay off your debt.

1. Complete your balance transfer ASAP. Most offers give you 60 days to transfer your balance over to the new card before you forfeit the promotional offer. However, your clock on the offer starts right away, so waiting 60 days means losing two months of your 0 percent promotional period.

2. Seriously, pause on this workbook right now and go complete the process of moving over your debt!

   I have completed my balance transfer. YES / NO

3. Always pay on time. Missing a payment due date could cause you to lose your promotional offer and get chucked into the penalty APR group, which is usually north of 20 percent. Set up autopay or put a reminder on your calendar to pay your bill.

4. Make a realistic, actionable plan to pay it off. Do the math and see how much you need to pay each month in order to hit debt freedom by the time your 0 percent promotional period ends.

$$\frac{\textbf{(Your balance owed + the balance transfer fee)}}{\textbf{Months of balance transfer offer}} = \textbf{Monthly payment to crush debt}$$

Example:

You owe $3,000. The balance transfer fee is 5% and lasts 18 months. 5% of $3,000 is $150.

$$\frac{\textbf{(\$3,150)}}{\textbf{18 months}} = \textbf{\$175 per month to pay off debt by end of the 18-month promotional period}$$

Your turn:

$$\frac{(\$\underline{\hspace{2cm}})}{\underline{\hspace{2cm}} \textbf{ months}} = \$\underline{\hspace{1cm}} \textbf{ monthly payment}$$

5. Don't spend on the card. Complete the balance transfer and stick that credit card in the literal or figurative freezer. Never swipe/insert/tap it to pay for a purchase! Don't add it to any of your digital wallets! Sure, the offer might say you have 0 percent APR on the transferred balance (or balances) *and* 0 percent APR on new purchases for a set period of time. This tactic is the bank equivalent of twirling a ridiculous mustache and tying your bank account to the railroad tracks. Spending on the card is an easy way to trip you up. Just keep things simple and don't spend on your balance transfer credit card.

6. Still have debt left? You may not receive a credit limit big enough to roll over all the debt on a single card (or multiple cards). Or maybe paying off your rollover before the end of the promotional period is impossible for your budget. That's okay. You can always roll over the remaining debt to a new balance transfer offer when your current one expires.

Helpful Hint: Reevaluate your plan as you go. For example, you decide to use a balance transfer and one of your credit card debts drops to 0% APR. You might be tempted to make that the bottom priority in your debt payoff because Debt Avalanche tells you to structure from highest interest rate to lowest. Now 0% APR makes it the lowest. In this case, you shouldn't doggedly pursue Debt Avalanche and instead focus resources on that 0% APR, because that means all your extra money is going toward aggressively paying off the principal balance of that debt!

Personal Loan

A personal loan is what's known as an installment loan. Just like a mortgage, an auto loan, or a student loan—you take out a loan with set terms about monthly payments in order to pay it off on a timeline. A personal loan can be used to finance a purchase you currently can't pay for in cash, which, yes, is creating debt. A personal loan can also be used to consolidate your debt into one easy payment with a lower interest rate. Similar to a balance transfer, you take out a new loan—with a lower interest rate—and use that to pay off an old loan or even multiple loans. This can help consolidate what was once multiple payments on different loans into one simple loan payment.

Credit cards often have double-digit interest rates into the twenties or even thirties. Personal loans can offer significantly lower interest rates in the single digits or low teens for eligible applicants. As detailed in the balance transfer section, lowering your interest rate can save you significant money and time on your debt payoff journey. In the next chapter, we'll discuss student loan refinancing, which offers a way to consolidate your student loans into one payment.

Going the personal loan route means having a built-in plan for when you'll be debt-free because the loan comes with a term. You make set monthly payments, and it's easier to understand exactly how much is going to the principal versus interest, unlike the complexities of paying down credit card debt.

A personal loan may look something like this: $5,000 for 24 months at 6 percent APR with a monthly payment of $221.60. Making that payment means you will be debt-free at the end of 24 months. You could even pay a little extra each month or make a few larger payments during the year (perhaps at bonus time) in order to pay off the loan before month 24.

What to Watch Out For

Personal loans are generally a bit less trap- and fee-riddled than balance transfers. However, there are still some ways lenders try to pad their pockets.

ORIGINATION FEE

An origination fee is a percentage of your loan that you pay when it's first disbursed. If you borrow $5,000 with a 3 percent origination fee, then your fee is $150. Often this fee is taken out of the loan before it's deposited into your bank account, which means you'd actually get $4,850 in your account.

PREPAYMENT PENALTY

Prepayment penalty fees are charged when you get aggressive about debt repayment and pay off your loan before the end of the term. Paying the loan early ticks off lenders because they're losing money—the interest you would've been charged had you hung on until the end of your term. Like the origination fee, it's not considered a shady practice if you understand it's part of the loan deal, but you can probably find a loan without prepayment penalties.

PRECOMPUTED INTEREST

Precomputed interest ensures that the lender still gets that sweet, sweet interest rate money even if you make large payments to aggressively pay down your debt quickly. The simple (aka normal) interest method will charge you based on the principal balance still owed each month. This is why paying off your debt early saves you money. Precomputed interest charges you interest based on the original terms of the loan. Making early or large payments up front just means more is going to interest initially, which ensures the lender still gets the interest payments he anticipated upon giving you the loan. Don't get a loan with precomputed interest if you plan to try to pay off the loan before the end of your term.

ADD-ON INSURANCE

The lender may try to sell you on additional policies for a monthly or annual fee, like unemployment or credit insurance, that is designed to help you if you can't pay the loan. It sounds like a great option, but do you really need to be paying a monthly premium for this protection in case you happen to lose your job during the term of your loan? Perhaps putting the cost of the premium in an emergency fund is a better use of your money.

PICK YOUR STRATEGY

Based on everything you just read, rank Debt Snowball, Debt Avalanche, balance transfer, and personal loan from most likely to work for you to least likely.

1. _____

2. _____

3. _____

4. _____

What does your plan look like with strategy #1?

I plan to use _____ to build my debt payoff plan.

Each month I can put $_____ extra toward my debt.

Based on how much I can put toward my debt, I should be debt-free in _____ months.

One major consideration is that you don't have to exclusively stick with one strategy, especially if it's not motivating you. Perhaps you said Debt Avalanche would be number one, but now you're three months in and you're getting frustrated by the lack of significant progress. Well, try switching to Debt Snowball and see if that makes you feel better!

EXERCISE
SUCCESS TRACKER

When my husband and I were working on paying off more than $50,000 in student loan debt, we found tracking our progress to be incredibly motivating. A debt payoff journey can be exhausting. Looking back at the progress you've made is excellent motivation when you feel like you're in a slump or it's just not happening fast enough.

Personally, I recommend you keep track of your progress with a spreadsheet in Excel or Google Sheets or your preferred platform. But feel free to use the grid below in the beginning or as inspiration to build your own.

TYPE OF DEBT	LENDER	MONTHLY PAYMENT	JANUARY BALANCE	FEBRUARY BALANCE	MARCH BALANCE	APRIL BALANCE	MAY BALANCE	JUNE BALANCE
		$	$	$	$	$	$	$
		$	$	$	$	$	$	$
		$	$	$	$	$	$	$
		$	$	$	$	$	$	$
		$	$	$	$	$	$	$
		$	$	$	$	$	$	$
		$	$	$	$	$	$	$
		$	$	$	$	$	$	$
		$	$	$	$	$	$	$

TYPE OF DEBT	LENDER	MONTHLY PAYMENT	JULY BALANCE	AUGUST BALANCE	SEPTEMBER BALANCE	OCTOBER BALANCE	NOVEMBER BALANCE	DECEMBER BALANCE
		$	$	$	$	$	$	$
		$	$	$	$	$	$	$
		$	$	$	$	$	$	$
		$	$	$	$	$	$	$
		$	$	$	$	$	$	$
		$	$	$	$	$	$	$
		$	$	$	$	$	$	$
		$	$	$	$	$	$	$
		$	$	$	$	$	$	$

GET YOUR FINANCIAL LIFE TOGETHER CHECK-IN

What is your biggest takeaway (or aha moment) from this chapter?

_____.

_____.

_____.

What feels most overwhelming about this chapter?

_____.

_____.

_____.

Why does it feel so overwhelming to you in this moment?

_____.

_____.

_____.

Based on what you just learned, write down one actionable step you can take this week to improve your financial life.

_____.

_____.

_____.

Chapter 9

Student Loans: How to Handle Them Without Having a Full-on Panic Attack

STUDENT LOANS ARE financial and emotional weights on so many of us. They impact millions and millions of Americans and yet it feels so easy to screw up, and there's little to no support on how to make the right steps.

Let's change that!

When I married my husband, our union came with the price tag of more than $50,000 in student loans. He'd already been diligently paying for several years before we got married, but it seemed like the balance just never went down. After we got married, we devised a plan to aggressively pay off those loans—but we also continued to live and enjoy life. It doesn't have to be an either/or situation. You can repay debt *and* continue to spend money doing things you love.

In this chapter, we're going to review different strategies you can use to build your own student loan repayment plan.

FEDERAL VS. PRIVATE STUDENT LOANS

Federal > Private.

It's a fact. Federal student loans are superior to private student loans. The government is a far more benevolent lender than private entities, which means you stand to receive certain perks on federal student loans. Those include access to income-driven repayment plans, forgiveness programs, cancellation of loans by the federal government, and, most notably in recent years, a long-term pause on payments during the COVID-19 pandemic.

Private lenders are simply not as generous, and there aren't any forgiveness programs. You have to pay back what you borrowed plus interest.

HOW THE HELL DO I FIND MY LOANS?

The federal government makes it pretty easy to track down your student loans. You need your Federal Student Aid (FSA) ID to log in (or create an account) at studentaid.gov/.

 Helpful Hint: It's important to keep track of your loans, because your loan servicers can (and probably will) change during your repayment journey. For example, in 2021 Navient decided to no longer service federal student loans. That left about six million borrowers to be matched with a new servicer. It's important to keep tabs on who owns your debt to ensure you're making payments to the right place. Of course you're supposed to be notified if this happens, but that's not always a flawless transition. . . .

Private student loans should be on your credit report, even if you've been in deferment and you aren't making payments yet. Remember from chapter 6 that you're entitled to a free copy of your credit reports from all credit bureaus once per year. AnnualCreditReport.com is a safe place to visit, or go directly to Experian, TransUnion, and Equifax.

EXERCISE
FACE YOUR NUMBERS (AGAIN): STUDENT LOAN EDITION

Fill in the grid on the following page with details about your student loans.

Helpful Hint: Don't forget to talk to your parents to see if there are any loans your parents have in their names that they expect you to help pay off.

LENDER	TYPE OF LOAN: PRIVATE/ FEDERAL	APR	MONTHLY PAYMENT DUE	TOTAL AMOUNT OWED	STATUS (CURRENT/ DEFERMENT/ FORBEARANCE/ DELINQUENT/DEFAULT)
		%	$	$	
		%	$	$	
		%	$	$	
		%	$	$	
		%	$	$	
		%	$	$	
		%	$	$	
		%	$	$	
		%	$	$	
		%	$	$	
		%	$	$	
		%	$	$	
		%	$	$	
		%	$	$	
		%	$	$	

DEALING WITH LOANS IN DELINQUENCY OR DEFAULT

In an ideal world, you would reach out to your lender *before* a missed payment and ask for a grace period or extension. (This usually works only once if you have a history of on-time payments.) But we aren't always in an ideal world!

It takes only one day. Your student loans are usually delinquent the day after you miss a payment. The loans stay delinquent until you're caught up. If you haven't paid after 90 days, your servicer will likely report the delinquency to the credit bureaus. That time period can be even shorter for private lenders.

Did something trip you up, and despite your long history of making on-time payments, did you suddenly miss one?

A goodwill letter that asks for forgiveness and shows a track record of on-time payments may convince the lender or servicer to remove the late payment from your credit report.

EXERCISE
WRITING A GOODWILL LETTER

[Your name]
[Return address]
[E-mail]
[Date]
[Loan company]
Re: Delinquency on Account #

To Whom It May Concern, / Hello, [name of loan company],

A nice salutation/greeting, background information on who you are, your account number, and how you realized you had a late payment.

_____.

_____.

_____.

Explain your history of on-time payments and the situation that led to you missing a payment.

_____.

_____.

_____.

Share how you've rectified the situation that led you to missing a payment and how you're able to get back on track and not miss any more payments.

_____.

_____.

_____.

Explain why it's important to you (and your credit history/score) that your credit remain strong. For example, applying for a mortgage or to refinance one, or for an auto loan or a new rental agreement.

_____.

_____.

_____.

Finally, close with a request to have a goodwill adjustment made and the late payment removed from your credit report. Be overly polite here! Words like "humbly request" certainly don't hurt.

_____.

_____.

_____.

Sincerely,

[Your name]

WHAT HAPPENS IF I DEFAULT?

Default will not only rip your credit history to shreds, but also:

- Revokes your ability to get deferment or forbearance or to enter into an income-driven repayment program.

- Your wages could be garnished to repay a loan.

- Your tax refund could be withheld to repay a federal loan.

- Collection agencies might start calling.

- You lose your eligibility to apply for any other federal student aid.

COSIGNED STUDENT LOANS

Do you have private student loans? Did your parents cosign on any of them? It's important that you understand the implications of cosigned student loans.

If you aren't able to pay, then the lender will collect from your parents (or whoever cosigned on the loan). Failure to pay not only damages your credit history but also starts to ding your parents' credit as well. Naturally, this has the potential to cause both emotional and financial problems for you and your parents.

What is the balance of your cosigned private student loans? $_____

Does your lender discharge in the case of death? Yes / No

There is a possibility that if you were to die prematurely, your parents would still be on the hook for paying off your student loans. Federal loans are discharged in the case of death, but not all private lenders offer this yet if there is a cosigner. Be sure to check your policy (or just call your lender and ask) to know if your parents would still be required to pay out the total. If the answer is yes, you should consider getting a term life insurance policy (not whole life—term!) that's large enough to cover the balance of your debt. Name your cosigners as the beneficiaries of the policy. This would ensure the cosigner would inherit enough money to cover the cost of repaying those loans and not cause financial harm to them upon your untimely death.

I know that's a bummer of a paragraph to read—but it is a critical consideration when your financial life is tied up with someone else's.

BUILDING YOUR STUDENT LOAN REPAYMENT PLAN

You've gathered all the information about your loans, so now it's time to actually build a plan! Your student loan repayment plan will probably be a mixture of a few different programs. Let's discuss your options so you can customize a plan that works best for you!

Income-Driven Repayment Plans

Many (but not all) federal student loans are eligible for income-driven repayment plans. These plans help make your monthly student loan payment more affordable by capping the amount you have to pay as a percentage of your discretionary income.

A formula is used to figure out your discretionary income and it is based on how much of your adjusted gross income exceeds the poverty line as determined by your state. (It's okay if your eyes just glazed over.) Luckily, this gets calculated for you!

There are four main income-driven repayment plans:

1. Revised Pay As You Earn (REPAYE)

2. Pay As You Earn (PAYE)

3. Income-Based Repayment (IBR)

4. Income-Contingent Repayment (ICR)

How Income-Driven Repayment Programs Work

First, you consolidate your federal loan through the Federal Direct Consolidation Loan (this is not refinancing!). Then you enroll in a repayment plan. There are regulations about which program you are eligible for based on when your loan was disbursed.

Once you are enrolled, your payments are capped at 10, 15, or 20 percent of your discretionary income, depending on your program. (Those were the rates at the time of writing. There have been proposals to cap at 5 percent, so check Studentaid.gov for the most recent information.) You continue to make monthly payments, and every year you recertify your eligibility. Your payments will change depending on if your life has changed (e.g., salary increases or decreases; you get married, have kids, etc.). If you still have debt after 20 to 25 years (depending on the program), then the remainder is discharged.

Helpful Hint: Don't pay to have a third party handle your federal student loans. There are plenty of predatory services offering to enroll you in a "new" payment plan or forgiveness program—for a fee, of course. You can enroll in any federal program for free. Save the money and put it toward your loans.

The Marriage Trap

Income impacts your monthly payment, and your tax returns are used to calculate your monthly payment. Getting married could significantly impact your monthly payments, especially if you file your tax return jointly with your spouse, because then it's not just your income, but also your spouse's that goes into the calculation.

It's about to get a little technical.

Let's use an example of two people who have loans on the REPAYE plan, Alex and Jo. Alex and Jo's monthly payment is capped at 10% of their discretionary income. To find discretionary income, the formula is:

(Annual income*) – (150% of the poverty guideline for your family size and state of residence)

Alex earns $55,000 and Jo earns $65,000. They live in Colorado (the 48 contiguous states and DC all have the same poverty guidelines). Even though they live together, they still each count as a family size of one because they aren't married and don't file taxes jointly. In 2022, the poverty guideline for a family of one is $13,590.

Alex's discretionary income: ($55,000) – (150% of $13,590, which is $20,385) = $34,615

Jo's discretionary income: ($65,000) – ($20,385) = $44,615

Being on REPAYE means Alex's and Jo's monthly payments are capped at 10% of their discretionary income.

Alex's monthly payment: ($34,615) × 10% = $3,461.50, divided by 12 months = $288.46

Jo's monthly payment: ($44,615) × 10% = $4,461.50, divided by 12 months = $371.79

But here's the catch: If Alex and Jo get married and file taxes jointly, then each other's income will be used to determine their discretionary income and monthly payment. Suddenly, it will go to both of them having monthly payments based off of $120,000 in annual income. However, the poverty guideline will also change because now they're a family of two. The 2022 poverty guideline for a family of two is $18,310.

($120,000) – (150% of $18,310, which is $27,465) = $92,535

($92,535) × 10% = $9,253.50 divided by 12 months = $771.13

And that could be $771.13 *per person* depending on student loan balances and the type of

---

* You should use the annual adjusted gross income on your latest tax return.

income-driven repayment plan. That's a huge jump from Alex's and Jo's original monthly payments.

But there's good news! According to Studentaid.gov, "Any time we use joint income to calculate your payment amount, we consider your spouse's federal student loan debt and prorate your payment based on your share of the combined federal student loan debt."* That's excellent if you both have student loans. If only one of you has student loans, then your payment won't be prorated to consider your spouse's and your monthly payment can go up significantly based on adding your spouse's income.

There's one final consideration (I told you this is technical). Some income-driven repayment plan payments will never be higher than what you'd pay on a standard 10-year repayment plan. REPAYE, however, isn't one of those plans. So if one or both of the people in a married couple are on REPAYE, then you should really research how much your monthly payment could increase. There are lots of online calculators to use to play around with your personal information, including one on Studentaid.gov.

It doesn't matter if you're both on income-driven repayment plans. Your incomes will mutually impact the other person's payments. Do the math and see if you can afford the potential increase in payments before legally saying, "I do!" Filing separately can sometimes negate the issue for PAYE and IBR plans, but that could have other tax cost implications and the government may close that loophole.

Am I Eligible for a Forgiveness Plan?

Federal student loans can be eligible for forgiveness programs.

The most well-known forgiveness program is Public Service Loan Forgiveness (PSLF). For starters, your loans need to be on an income-driven repayment plan. Then you are able to have the remaining balance on your Direct Loans forgiven after 120 qualifying monthly payments *and* working full-time for a qualifying employer. As the name implies, you must work in public service, which includes government organizations and not-for-profit organizations.

There are also a Teacher Loan Forgiveness Program and discharge options for circumstances like closed schools or total and permanent disability.

Learn more about current forgiveness program options at Studentaid.gov.

---

*https://studentaid.gov/articles/4-things-to-know-about-marriage/.

Certain states also help pay off student loans, so be sure to do your research to see if any programs are available to you.

Should I Refinance My Student Loans?

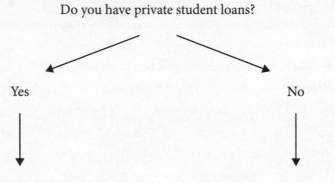

Do you have private student loans?

Yes

No

You should explore refinancing options

You probably don't need to refinance

Helpful Hint: You don't have to refinance all of your loans. For example, some may be federal on income-driven repayment plans, while others are private with high interest rates. You can refinance the private loans and leave the federal ones alone on the income-driven repayment plans.

Consequences of Refinancing Federal Student Loans
Refinancing federal loans turns them into private loans. That means you will give up the perks associated with federal loans. You won't have the option for income-driven repayment programs. No student loan forgiveness. No deferment or forbearance. It's game over. And much like accidentally leaving a red T-shirt in with your white laundry, there is no reversing the consequences.

What Exactly Is Refinancing?

Refinancing is much like the balance transfers we discussed in chapter 8. You take out a new loan to pay off the old loan. The new loan is at a lower interest rate, which means you can pay off your debt faster.

For example, your student loans carry a 7.05 percent APR and are being serviced by Bank BleedingYouDry. Bank WeCareALittleMore is willing to offer you a rate of 3.50 percent if you move your debt over. So you take out the loan with Bank WeCareALittleMore and pay off the loan at Bank BleedingYouDry. You now just have the new loan at Bank WeCareALittleMore with a 3.50 percent APR, which means you can pay it off both faster and with less interest.

Most lenders offering refinancing want you to have achieved the following:

- Have a 700+ credit score.

- Have been employed for at least a year.

- Have made at least six months of payments on your student loans.

- Never missed a payment nor had loans in default.

Helpful Hint: Go with a fixed interest rate and not a variable rate. Variable rates are usually lower at first, but have the potential to hike above a fixed rate. Unless you plan to pay off your debt before a potential rate change, it's best to stick with fixed.

What Are My Options If I Didn't Graduate but Have Student Loans?

Unfortunately, carrying student loans without a degree is one of the toughest situations for repayment options. Federal loans could still be put on an income-driven repayment plan, but private loans are tough to handle, as refinancing is likely not an option; lenders typically include having a degree as part of the underwriting criteria. Instead, you can focus on your own ways to boost your student loan repayment plan.

Other Ways to Boost Your Student Loan Repayment Plan

Booster 1: Pay Above the Minimum

Student loan payments are designed to get you to repay the principal balance plus interest during a set period of time (often 10 years). Every little bit you pay above the monthly payment will help shave time off your overall repayment journey.

In fact, a mere $10 more a month could save you hundreds of dollars and reduce how long you're paying off those loans. This should sound familiar from the Debt Snowball and Debt Avalanche work we did in chapter 8. If you skipped that, consider going back and doing those exercises first.

EXERCISE
BOOSTING YOUR MONTHLY PAYMENT

Step 1: Write down your student loans in the order you'd like to prioritize paying them off.

Here are a few ideas:

- You can use the Debt Snowball (smallest to highest balance) or Debt Avalanche (highest to lowest interest rate) strategies from chapter 8.

- You can create a hybrid of Snowball and Avalanche by picking high-interest loans with smaller balances, which saves money but still helps you get that motivating win.

- You can prioritize the one that annoys you the most as motivation to knock it out quickly.

This is completely your call.

Step 2: Based on the cash flow work you did in chapter 3 and chapter 8, how much extra per month could you put toward your debts?

I can put $_____ extra toward my monthly payments.

Step 3: Add that extra money you can easily free up right now to the Goal Monthly Payment of your #1 debt to pay off and put a date for this month.

Step 4: Future Goal Monthly Payments can be based on the Debt Snowball or Debt Avalanche strategies. You would simply add the amount of the Goal Monthly Payment to the next line's Monthly Payment.

RANK	LENDER	MONTHLY PAYMENT DUE	GOAL MONTHLY PAYMENTS
1	Bank A	$120	$150
2	Bank B	$110	$260*

*$150 + $110 = $260

You will have paid off the first loan before adding the Goal Monthly Payment of $150 to the $110 monthly payment due for the second loan.

Step 5: Challenge yourself by setting dates for when you want to start making the goal payments for each loan. Remember, that means you will have paid off the preceding loan!

⚠ *Don't forget to keep making the minimum monthly payments on all your loans. Failure to do so will result in delinquency and then default.*

RANK	LENDER	MONTHLY PAYMENT DUE	GOAL MONTHLY PAYMENTS	DATE FOR GOAL PAYMENTS
1		$	$	_____/_____/20_____
2		$	$	_____/_____/20_____
3		$	$	_____/_____/20_____
4		$	$	_____/_____/20_____
5		$	$	_____/_____/20_____
6		$	$	_____/_____/20_____
7		$	$	_____/_____/20_____
8		$	$	_____/_____/20_____
9		$	$	_____/_____/20_____
10		$	$	_____/_____/20_____
11		$	$	_____/_____/20_____
12		$	$	_____/_____/20_____
13		$	$	_____/_____/20_____
14		$	$	_____/_____/20_____
15		$	$	_____/_____/20_____

Booster 2: Tell Your Servicer to Apply Any Extra Payment to Principal Debt
Your loan servicer can do something a little sneaky once you start to make those extra payments above your monthly minimum.

Instead of applying that extra money to your principal balance, your loan servicer can apply it: first, to outstanding fees; second, to interest (including future interest); and third, to your principal balance, which doesn't help you get out of debt efficiently. This is especially true if you have more than one loan with the servicer, because your servicer is probably spreading the love around instead of applying those extra payments where it's most beneficial for you. The best way to use your extra payment will be to focus it on one loan specifically instead of spreading it across the balances you owe.

Helpful Hint: You might see that you start owing "$0" a month because your extra payments have added up enough that you've paid ahead and covered the interest accrued since your last payment. Keep making payments. If you stop, then you'll just end up accruing interest again.

EXERCISE
STAND UP FOR YOURSELF:
TELL YOUR SERVICER WHAT YOU WANT

Here's the plan of attack to counteract this devilish plot:

Step 1: Decide which loan should be receiving the extra money (aka refer to the last exercise!).

Step 2: You can call your servicer and request that they put the surplus of your payment toward the principal balance but it's always a good idea to have it in writing as well.

Send your servicer a formal letter via e-mail or snail mail stating how you want any additional amount over your minimum payment to be applied. For example, it might say "to the highest interest rate debt first" or "to the debt with the smallest balance."

Here is a template for a formal letter to send inspired by the Consumer Financial Protection Bureau's (CFPB) template.

Important Note: You should modify any of the items in the list below based on how you are actually paying off your debt. This letter is based on someone using the Debt Snowball method and focusing on smallest balance debts first, but with a dash of Debt Avalanche as noted in step 2.

[Your name]
[Return address]
[E-mail]
[Date]
[Loan company]
Re: [account number for the loan, if you have it]

To Whom It May Concern, / Hello, [name of loan company],

Below, please find instructions for how to apply payments I make that are greater than the minimum amount due.

1. After applying the minimum amount due for each loan, any additional amount should be applied to the loan with the lowest balance first.

2. If there are multiple loans with the same balance, please apply the additional amount to the loan with the highest interest rate.

3. If any additional amount above the minimum amount due ends up paying off an individual loan, please then apply the remainder of my payment to the loan with the next lowest balance.

If any third party makes a payment toward my loans on my behalf, you should follow the instructions listed above. Please apply these instructions to all future payments or provide an explanation as to why you are unable to do so.

Thank you for your cooperation.

Sincerely,
[Your name]

Customize the letter with your own rules based on your preferred repayment strategy.

1. _____

   _____

   _____

2. _____

   _____

   _____

3. _____

   _____

   _____

You should send this request via certified mail if you send a letter and/or follow up shortly afterward to ensure that it was received.

Step 3: Track your loans each month to ensure that the payments are being applied properly and that your principal balances are actually starting to decrease.

Step 4: Keep making those aggressive payments on a set schedule, even when you see that it's $0 due (despite still having a principal balance) or that your payment due date is suddenly months away.

Booster 3: Opt for Biweekly Payments

If you get paid on a biweekly schedule, then you probably know that two months a year you get those sweet, sweet three-paycheck months. Using the same principle, you can also leverage the weeks in a year to squeeze out an extra student loan payment with no pain to you! All it takes is properly splitting up your student loan payments.

Some, though unfortunately not all, lenders allow you to set up biweekly payments. You'll pay your student loan twice a month instead of once.

Don't worry. This doesn't mean you pay the minimum due twice. Instead, you split it in half.

For example, if you owe $400 a month, then you'll pay $200 in week 2 and $200 in week 4, for a total of $400. Using this repayment strategy actually forces you to make 26 biweekly payments, or 13 payments a year, instead of 12.

It's a simple strategy to give your repayments an extra boost, but impactful only if you're sure to pay the second half of your payment *before* your monthly due date. Due dates aren't always the last day of the month, so it can be easy to accidentally screw up and miss paying half your bill.

EXERCISE
PLOT OUT YOUR BIWEEKLY PAYMENTS

Fill in the grid on the next page to design your own biweekly payment strategy.

LENDER	MONTHLY PAYMENT DUE	BIWEEKLY PAYMENT AMOUNT	MONTHLY DUE DATE	BIWEEKLY PAYMENT #1 DUE DATE	BIWEEKLY PAYMENT #2 DUE DATE
	$	$	___/___/20___	___/___/20___	___/___/20___
	$	$	___/___/20___	___/___/20___	___/___/20___
	$	$	___/___/20___	___/___/20___	___/___/20___
	$	$	___/___/20___	___/___/20___	___/___/20___
	$	$	___/___/20___	___/___/20___	___/___/20___
	$	$	___/___/20___	___/___/20___	___/___/20___
	$	$	___/___/20___	___/___/20___	___/___/20___
	$	$	___/___/20___	___/___/20___	___/___/20___
	$	$		___/___/20___	___/___/20___
	$	$		___/___/20___	___/___/20___
	$	$		___/___/20___	___/___/20___
	$	$		___/___/20___	___/___/20___
	$	$		___/___/20___	___/___/20___
	$	$		___/___/20___	___/___/20___
	$				___/___/20___

What if your lender doesn't accept biweekly payments? Well, you could just give your own boost by paying your monthly payment due + the amount of a biweekly payment in the months you get those three paychecks (assuming you're paid biweekly).

NOW GO DEFEAT THOSE STUDENT LOANS

Mix and match the tools outlined in this chapter and chapter 8 to create the best strategy in your personal student loan situation. There's some perfect combination of extra payments, refinancing, income-driven repayment plans, and side hustling out there to help crush your student loans. At the very least, challenge yourself to add an extra $10 a month to one of your student loan payments as a way to get started!

- -

Get Your Financial Life Together Check-In

What is your biggest takeaway (or aha moment) from this chapter?

_____.

_____.

_____.

What feels the most overwhelming about this chapter?

_____.

_____.

_____.

Why does it feel so overwhelming to you in this moment?

_____ .

_____ .

_____ .

Based on what you just learned, write down one actionable step you can take this week to improve your financial life.

_____ .

_____ .

_____ .

Chapter 10

Life Is Already Overwhelmingly Expensive. Do I Really Have to Focus on Saving?

WHEN WAS THE last time an unexpected expense popped up? You know what I mean. Those new tires for your car, or your dog needed to get rushed to the vet, or a family member got sick and you had to book a last-minute flight, or your friend turned into a wedding monster and being in the bridal party cost way more than you anticipated.

My latest unexpected expense was _____

*and it cost me $*_____.

Life is full of moments that fall outside of our budgets—some of which can be joyful moments and some of which are frustrating or painful. It's easy to let other people's asks or our own desires dictate how we spend, save, and invest our money. That's why it's critical to adhere to the cliché yet true personal finance advice to pay yourself first.

LET'S GET THE CLICHÉ OUT OF THE WAY: PAY YOURSELF FIRST

What percentage of your paycheck goes toward savings *before* hitting your checking account?

_____%

How much money do you put into savings every month?

$_____

If you're struggling to answer either question, it's probably because the amount you save each month isn't consistent and fluctuates based on how much you have "left over" to put into savings at the end of the month. It's time to change this behavior.

"Pay yourself first" is the rallying cry of personal finance experts. It means the first thing you do with a paycheck is to save a chunk instead of waiting until the end of the month and hoping there is some left over.

Those with direct deposit paychecks can easily set up a percentage of each paycheck to automatically be routed into a savings account so it doesn't even hit your checking account first. (Just chat with HR or a manager if you're unclear about how to do this in your company portal. Self-employed folks like myself need to set up their own system, which could involve having a savings account at an entirely separate bank from your checking so you aren't tempted to constantly skim money out!) Automating your savings directly to a savings account takes the temptation to spend away.

Paying yourself first also implies that you have some understanding of your cash flow, which means that, yes, you must set a budget. A detailed understanding of how much is coming in and how much is going out enables you to find where it's possible to redirect money toward your savings goals.

There's no harm in starting small with your savings, like $10 per paycheck. Saving less than what it costs to buy a craft cocktail in most cities may sound completely pointless, but it's more about forming the habit.

Helpful Hint: Once you start living with 10 fewer dollars each month, you just adapt. The same then goes for $20, $50, even $100. Starting the process with a small amount and doing it gradually reduces the pinch and makes it easier to keep saving.

Paying yourself first is important, but I already get a sense that you might have a nagging voice in your head that's trying to undermine me (and you)! Let's address the elephant in the room. . . .

I'VE GOT DEBT, SO WHY SHOULD I CARE ABOUT SAVING?

"Yeah, okay," your brain might be thinking in your most sarcastic voice. While paying yourself first sounds great in theory, it seems absolutely ridiculous when you're looking at your credit card statement, student loan payment, rent bill, and all those other pesky money drains like feeding yourself. You feel fortunate enough to just break even at the end of the month, let alone start the month by tucking money away in an account you aren't supposed to touch.

Well, too bad.

Saving money prevents you from sinking deeper into debt by providing a buffer when you hit a streak of bad luck and everything you own suddenly breaks. The other option is to finance your emergencies on a credit card and begin or continue the downward spiral of high interest and a principal balance that refuses to decrease.

It is important to strike the almighty balance between paying off debt *and* starting to build savings.

My total debt is $_____.

My totals savings are $ _____.

There are so many goals for which you might be saving, but the foundation of your savings strategy—no matter your debt situation—should be your emergency fund.

THE FIRST SAVINGS ACCOUNT YOU NEED: AN EMERGENCY FUND

The emergency fund is just part of your overall savings strategy. Yes, you should have goals beyond a fully funded emergency savings account, like a down payment or dream vacation, but the emergency fund is a foundational part of your financial journey. Debt or no debt, it serves as your parachute when the budget busters strike and leave your bank account drained. Murphy's Law naturally suggests the opportune time for such an attack to occur is exactly when you've just maxed out your credit card and need to wait another two weeks for a paycheck.

Classic financial wisdom advises that you have at least six months of living expenses as a sound buffer against the threat of the unexpected, but alas, that can be quite unrealistic early on in establishing your financial footing.

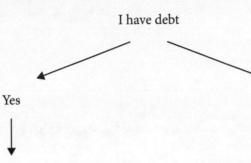

Helpful Hint: You might have read that $1,000 is how much you should have if you're paying off debt (which I unfortunately agreed with when I wrote my first book back in 2016). But I changed my mind, and that was before a global pandemic. Frankly, $1,000 just isn't enough, which is why you should have at least one month of bare essential living expenses.

Guidelines for Building Your Emergency Fund

I have debt

Yes

No

One month of bare essential living expenses (if it's just you). Whether it's student loans, consumer debt, or a fun mix, you need to have at least one month of bare essential living expenses squirreled away for when you get hit upside the head with the unexpected. And it's going to happen. If you have dependents, even a pet, I recommend adding another $500 to that number. Things are going to unexpectedly happen to loved ones too.

Or your debt is highly manageable, low-interest debt: **6 months of living expenses: Yes, the common advice still stands.** Know how much you need to cover a month of bare essential living expenses—your thrice-a-week happy hours might need to get nixed in this scenario—and have at least six months of that number in liquid savings. That means not invested in the stock market, and not socked away in your company 401(k), just sitting pretty in your savings account. When everything goes sideways, you really don't want to have to deal with selling off investments to pay rent.

This all sounds nice, but I have variable (or unpredictable) income!

↓

9 months of living expenses: Everything is more expensive when you're your own boss. Health care, taxes, and even saving are up to you. And working with a variable income is stressful, so it makes sense to pad your emergency savings fund with more than you would as a traditional office employee.

And seriously, if that money isn't in a high-interest savings account, then flip back to chapter 5 for a refresher!

EXERCISE
CREATE YOUR BARE ESSENTIALS BUDGET

It's overwhelming to save up a month or three months or six months of living expenses. That can be a lot of money—depending on your needs. But one important reframe here is that you are simply looking at the *bare essentials.* Your emergency fund isn't based on your living expenses when you can indulge in dinners out, buying craft supplies, happy hour, traveling, or whatever your indulgences may be. Your emergency fund is based on your bare essential budget.

How much do you need to cover your bare essential living expenses each month?
Fill in the grids on the following pages to figure out your grand total for a single month.
In the grids, fill in the costs of your *monthly* payments for each item.
Total up the cost of each section and then add it all up for a grand total at the end.

A Note About Annual Expenses: Some of the expenses below might be billed annually (e.g., car registration or insurance), so you should look up the annual cost and divide by 12 to know how much per month you should be setting aside to prepare for payment.

For example, Erin pays $550 per year on renter's insurance.

$$\frac{(\$550)}{12 \text{ months}} = \$45.83 \text{ per month}$$

Erin will budget $46 per month and set it aside into an account for bills to be prepared for the annual payment when it's due.

HOUSING

Rent/mortgage	
HOA/Coop/Condo fee	
Property taxes*	

TOTAL $_____

* Property taxes may be bundled into your mortgage payment.

UTILITIES

Electric	
Internet/cable	
Water	
Gas	
Home phone	
Cell phone	

TOTAL $_____

TRANSPORTATION

Public transit pass	
Auto loan	
Gas	
Insurance	
Registration	
Parking	

TOTAL $_____

FOOD

Groceries	
Pet food	
Dining out/meal kits*	

TOTAL $_____

* Generally not advised if you're paring down to the bare minimum, but if this is essential to you for possibly the time saved, that's a consideration.

HOUSEHOLD GOODS & TOILETRIES

Toilet paper	
Cleaning supplies	
Shampoo, deodorant, soap	
Makeup	
Sanitary products	
Other	

TOTAL $_____

DEBT (COST OF YOUR MINIMUM MONTHLY PAYMENTS)

Credit cards	
Student loans	
Miscellaneous debt (medical, legal, etc.)	
Personal loan	

TOTAL $_____

MEDICINE

Human	
Pet	
Copays*	

TOTAL $_____

If you know you or a family member will need to be going to the doctor frequently, then it's prudent to include copays in your bare essentials budget.

CHILDREN

Childcare	
Diapers/wipes	
Clothing/shoes	
Activities*	

TOTAL $_____

Activities likely need to be cut, however, you can also determine if an exception should be made, such as for a high schooler who is a competitive athlete and may get a scholarship.

INSURANCE PREMIUMS

Life	
Health	
Renter's/homeowner's	
Other	

TOTAL $_____

MISCELLANEOUS

Other monthly payments you make (e.g., spousal support, family support, tithing, etc.).

TOTAL $_____

GRAND TOTAL $_____

EXERCISE
EMERGENCY SAVINGS FUND TRACKER

Charting your progress is such a powerful way to stay motivated! Consider tearing out the next page and posting it where you can see it on a regular basis as you work toward your goal.

Each piggy bank represents:

$_____ toward my goal of $_____.

Color in a piggy bank each time you progress toward your goal.

OTHER SAVINGS GOALS

An emergency fund is the start, but it's certainly not the only reason you have a savings goal. There are short-, medium-, and long-term savings goals. Short term is a few months to 3 years. Medium term is 4 to 9 years and long term is 10+ years. Granted, there is some gray area between longer-term medium goals and shorter long-term goals.

Short-term goals often include vacations, weddings, building that emergency fund, or buying an item you've been coveting.

Medium-term goals (depending on your age/timeline) include a down payment for a home, buying a new car, or starting a business.

Long-term goals include saving for a child's college fund or setting aside money to help your parents as they age or for your retirement.

It's important to set a timeline for your goal because it helps determine how you should save.

For long-term goals, like retirement, you should actually be investing your money instead of letting it sit in a savings account. The timing also helps dictate how to best prioritize your goals.

EXERCISE
SET STRONG, ACTIONABLE SAVINGS GOALS

There are four essential parts of setting a strong, actionable savings goal.

1. What do you want?
   Write down exactly what you want and be specific. "I want to save $5,000 in the next two years to take a trip to Japan." "I want to save $25,000 for a down payment on a house in the next five years."

2. **Nickname**
   Create a nickname for this savings goal.

3. **Amount**
   How much do you need?

4. **Deadline**
   Set a date for when you want to accomplish your goal.

GOAL	NICKNAME	AMOUNT	DEADLINE
		$	____/____/20____
		$	____/____/20____
		$	____/____/20____
		$	____/____/20____
		$	____/____/20____

Once you have all this information, you can then start to figure out how it works into your monthly budget.

EXERCISE
HOW MUCH SHOULD YOU SAVE EACH MONTH?

Well, it depends! Of course it does. Because it depends on your goals!

This exercise walks you through the incredibly simple math of determining how much you need to save each month to reach your financial goal.

Savings Calculation:

(amount) ÷ (months until deadline) = monthly savings goal

For example, you want to take that trip to Japan in two years. You estimate it will cost you $5,000.

That means ($5,000) ÷ (24 months) = $208.33 per month needs to be saved to reach your goal.

Now use the information from the previous exercise to run your savings calculations!

($_____ for _____ goal) ÷ (_____ months until deadline) =

$ _____ savings per month

($_____ for _____ goal) ÷ (_____ months until deadline) =

$ _____ savings per month

($_____ for _____ goal) ÷ (_____ months until deadline) =

$ _____ savings per month

($_____ for _____ goal) ÷ (_____ months until deadline) =

$ _____ savings per month

($_____ for _____ goal) ÷ (_____ months until deadline) =

$ _____ savings per month

EXERCISE
HOW TO PRIORITIZE YOUR SAVINGS GOALS

Wow, we've talked about a lot of different types of savings goals! You might even be feeling overwhelmed about the sheer number of accounts you want to set up right now. That's totally normal. There is one critical truth, though: You probably *don't* want to divide up the love evenly. In fact, it's probably important to prioritize some goals over others. This exercise will help you determine how to prioritize your savings goals.

Step 1: Look back at your list of goals. Determine if a goal is a need or a want. An emergency fund is a need. A vacation is a want. Needs will outrank wants when we prioritize. (Emergency funds and retirement accounts should be on your list!)

Step 2: How quickly do you want to achieve your goal? How flexible is the deadline? Are you willing to extend the length of time it will take to achieve your goal in order to prioritize something else?

Step 3: It's okay if one of the goals is getting $0 in monthly contributions for a period of time because you're focused on another goal. Or you can use it as motivation to figure out how to supercharge your earnings.

Note: It's important to reassess your savings goals at least twice a year. As life changes, your priorities (usually) should too!

PRIORITY	NICKNAME	AMOUNT	DEADLINE	MONTHLY CONTRIBUTION
1		$		$
2		$		$
3		$		$
4		$		$
5		$		$

A HANDFUL OF SAVINGS HACKS

Who doesn't love a good hack? When it comes to saving, there are a few strategies that can help nudge you toward your goals. Try implementing at least two of these within the next month and check them off when you do.

❑ Nickname accounts

You were asked to give your goals a nickname in the "Set Strong, Actionable Goals" exercise. Did you know that most banks and credit unions allow you to nickname your accounts? Instead of something meaningless like "Account 393840"—you could change it to "Quit My Job 2027." The more specific you can get, the better. This small little tweak just might help you avoid the temptation to skim money out of your savings account. The nickname serves as a reminder about why you're saving and why you should just leave that money alone!

❑ High-interest savings account

High(er)-interest savings accounts aren't going to make you rich, but every extra dollar toward your goal counts! Unfortunately, interest rates on savings accounts are a little volatile. It used to be common to see 1% APY and then 2% APY—but it tumbled back down closer to 0.50% APY in the very early 2020s. Then we started to see a rally back above 1.00% and all the way up above 2.00% in 2022. While rates will continue to go up and down, even a low 0.50% APY is better than the common 0.01% at many big banks. Go back to chapter 5 for a refresher on picking better financial products if your savings account APY has a zero after a decimal point!

❏ Incremental increases
In an ideal world, what percentage of your income do you want to be putting into savings?

_____%

It's okay if you can't contribute a big chunk of money toward your goals right away. Instead, focus on increasing the amount you're currently putting toward your savings (or investing) goal by 0.5% or 1% every few months. If you're doing 3% today, then try to do 4% next month and 5% in four to six months. That way the change will feel minimal as you ease your way toward your goal.

❏ Out of sight (but not out of mind)
Put your savings in an account you don't see when you log in to your main checking account. This probably means using a different bank entirely. The out-of-sight-out-of-mind principle will apply when you feel a bit strapped for cash. (Except I never want it to be totally out of mind, just harder to access at the moment.) This way your savings aren't sitting right in front of you, saying, "Hey, you can take some from here!" and it's easier to let it continue to accumulate.

❏ Find where to slash
Struggling to figure out places to reduce your spending? Pull six months' worth of credit card and bank statements and go through every single line item. Highlight any item (especially monthly subscriptions) that could be slashed or negotiated for a better rate.

❏ Save your savings
How often have you used a coupon or shopped a deal or negotiated on a bill and thought "Wow, I just saved $X?" But then what happens to those savings? They

probably just stay sitting in your checking account waiting to be spent! Be sure to actually save your savings by moving that money into a savings account!

EXERCISE
SIDE HUSTLE BRAINSTORM

There is a lot of emphasis about cutting out when we talk about savings. Cut those lattes, that avocado toast, after-work happy hour, those wax appointments, getting your hair and nails done—anything that's seen as "an indulgence." Sure, stripping our lives of joy and putting money away is one way to reach savings goals quickly. But there is another option.

You can spend less or you can focus on earning more.

Set a timer for 5 minutes and spend this time just brainstorming ways you can earn more money. It could be a one-off strategy (like a yard sale) or an ongoing business like selling scarves that you knit.

⚠️ *Warning: Multi-level marketing (MLM) schemes are rampant and often positioned as a way to earn money from home or a side hustle. It is rare that people truly make a strong net profit from an MLM (net profit means the money you earn after all the costs of doing business—in this case, usually buying product). The start-up costs are high. Please avoid using an MLM as a way to supplement your earnings. Unclear if you're being pitched an MLM? Investigate how you earn money and if you'd be required to recruit people in order to move up.*

Opportunities in my community:

_____.

_____.

_____.

If I had a small boutique shop, I would sell:

_____.

_____.

_____.

Skills I have that could be a side hustle opportunity:

_____.

_____.

_____.

How much I'd like to earn from a side hustle each month:

$_____

What could I do this week if I needed to try to make money quickly?

_____.

_____.

_____.

Helpful Hint: The money you earn from side hustling can also be put toward debt repayment instead of savings if that's your more significant money goal right now.

"WHAT IF" SAVINGS ACCOUNTS

One of the most poignant concepts about life paths is that our choices are rarely between good and bad options, because that would make the selection simple. We often have to decide between two good (or potentially life-altering) options. Do you take a risk and move to that city where you've always wanted to live or stay in your current town, where you have roots and established friendships? Do you adopt the dog you've wanted or keep your current (more flexible) lifestyle?

We all have "What If" paths in our minds. What are some of yours?

_____.

_____.

_____.

_____.

_____.

Other "What If" moments are less life altering, but still potentially expensive. For example, my husband, whom I affectionately call Peach, is a huge fan of the Buffalo Bills football team.

The last time the Bills went to the Super Bowl (well, at least as of this writing) was in 1994, when my husband was three years old. Because of this, he has a whole dream to go to the AFC Championship Game (the game that would qualify them to get to the Super Bowl) and then fly to Buffalo to watch the actual Super Bowl with his family. The point is, it would cost us quite a bit of money if—I should say "when"—the Bills make it back to the Super Bowl.

It would be a pretty big pain to completely reorganize our budget or try to reallocate funds from other trips in order to make his dream come true. So a few years ago, we started a "What If" savings account called the "Bills Dream Fund." We put a little bit of money aside each month into this account with the thought that it will subsidize most, if not all, of the trip by the time the Bills make his dream come true.

Another "What If" savings account my husband and I set up is for the possibility of expanding our family beyond us and our dog. Deciding to have a child is a major decision both emotionally and financially. The "What If" account is able to offset some of the financial anxiety around that decision by setting money aside that could be used for pregnancy and delivery costs if we ultimately decided to have a kid. Then, if we don't, it can be redirected toward investments or other short-term goals.

The "What If" Savings Account Provides the Luxury of Choice

The "What If" savings account is really a 2.0-level financial move. It's a way to start planning for possible realities after you're in a position to have your other bases, and short-term wants, covered. It's likely that this account functions to provide the illusion of control over what may happen in the future, but it's still another way to feel stable in your financial life and to lay the groundwork for spontaneous moments or simply changing your mind. It's also totally okay if this type of account doesn't appeal to how your brain works or sound necessary to you! I'll be honest: It's a great move for my fellow type A personalities out there!

There is one catch here: These should be short-term goals. Should your "What If" moment be five or ten years away (or more), then you should probably consider investing some of the money and not having it all tied up in cash savings.

Think about your own "What If" goals and fill in the table on the next page.

"WHAT IF" GOAL	PREDICTED AMOUNT NEEDED	TENTATIVE DATE
	$	_____/_____/20_____
	$	_____/_____/20_____
	$	_____/_____/20_____
	$	_____/_____/20_____
	$	_____/_____/20_____

Helpful Hint: "What If" savings accounts should be a fairly low priority because they're a way to hedge against the unexpected. Only if the "What If" turns into an "I Want" or "I Need" should it begin to potentially outrank other savings goals.

EXERCISE
CHECKLIST: BECOMING A STRONGER SAVER

Read through the checklist below and write down dates for when you want to accomplish these goals.

❏ Don't spend whatever you have left over at the end of month; instead, be proactive and pay yourself first. _____/_____/20_____

❏ Start small, and don't be discouraged if you can afford to save only $5 or $10 a month. _____/_____/20_____

❏ Automate so you aren't tempted to spend the money before you save.

_____/_____/20_____

❏ Put the money you're saving into an account you don't check daily or even

weekly. _____/_____/20_____

❏ Slash excess spending or pick up a side hustle to find money to pad your savings

account. _____/_____/20_____

❏ Gradually increase how much you save every few months, and be sure to increase

it when you get a raise to avoid completely succumbing to lifestyle inflation.

_____/_____/20_____

❏ Use part of your holiday bonus or tax return or any unexpected sum of money to

help beef up your savings. _____/_____/20_____

❏ Know your bare essential budget and have at least one month saved in an

emergency fund to start and ultimately up to six or nine months of bare essential

expenses. _____/_____/20_____

SAVING MAY NOT HAPPEN AS QUICKLY AS YOU WANT, BUT IT WILL HAPPEN

Building a healthy savings account doesn't happen in a few weeks or months, and in some cases it may take years. Just remember, it's always important to have savings, even if you're currently struggling with debt. It's okay if you feel demoralized if you can barely afford to contribute more than the cost of a latte into your savings account at first, but it's building the habit that matters. As you begin to pay down debt and also earn more, then you can start to contribute larger sums to your savings.

Get Your Financial Life Together Check-In

What is your biggest takeaway (or aha moment) from this chapter?

_____

_____

_____

What feels the most overwhelming about this chapter?

_____

_____

_____

Why does it feel so overwhelming to you in this moment?

_____

_____

_____

Based on what you just learned, write down one actionable step you can take this week to improve your financial life.

_____.

_____.

_____.

Chapter 11

I Can't Afford to Split This Dinner Bill Evenly! Navigating Finances and Friendship

YOUR BUDGET NEVER FAILS, your emergency savings is fully funded, and you're on top of investing for retirement and generally feeling like a financial badass. You can be absolutely flawless in your financial life, but if you allow other people to keep spending your money, you'll find that the foundation you've built for yourself is shaky.

Yes, that's the terrible secret of adulthood: It's incredibly easy to allow other people to spend our money.

Peer pressure, societal pressure, or just an inability to say no leads to lots of financial pain. Let's focus on how to set healthy, successful boundaries with friends when it comes to joining in on social engagements.

EXERCISE
RANT IT OUT

We've all had moments of feeling pressured to spend money we didn't want to. It could be a result of attending an event (e.g., bachelor/ette parties, weddings, birthday dinners, group trips), or it could be a flippant comment from a friend ("Your purse looks pretty worn down. You should get a new one"), or it could be just general social pressure to keep up or fit in ("We're going for happy hour after work. Want to come?").

Sometimes these moments can roll off our backs—but others stick with us. They can fester and ultimately even cause damage to our friendships.

Take the space below to rant about a moment when you spent money you didn't want to (or couldn't afford to) because of a friendship dynamic.

_____.

_____.

_____.

_____.

_____.

Woof, I bet it feels good to get that off your chest!

But you know I can't let you get away with just ranting about the situation. It's time to assess what could've been done differently.

Reread your story and reflect back on the lead-up to the moment when you felt (directly or indirectly) pressured by a friend to spend money.

What could you have said or done differently?

_____.

_____.

_____.

When would've been a good moment to draw a financial boundary?

_____.

_____.

_____.

What would you have been comfortable sharing about your own financial life to give your friend context about why you needed to draw that boundary?

_____.

_____.

_____.

How would you probably feel today about the situation if you'd drawn that boundary back then?

_____.

_____.

_____.

While I was writing *Broke Millennial Talks Money: Scripts, Stories, and Advice to Navigate Awkward Financial Conversations*, one quote from an interviewee really stuck with me:

You have to weigh which will win out: the embarrassment or the resentment. Is it going to be more embarrassing to own up to your financial situation or will you be resentful for three days because you said yes when you really can't afford it?

—Melanie Lockert, author of *Dear Debt* and host of the
Mental Health & Wealth Show podcast

This is an incredibly powerful way to reframe a moment of potential embarrassment or awkwardness. Resentment is much more likely to linger and fester and damage your friendships.

HOW TO ACTUALLY SET BOUNDARIES WITH FRIENDS

The only way to set healthy and effective boundaries with your friends is to communicate with them. No amount of passive-aggressive behavior or complaining with another friend or silently simmering with low-grade rage is going to draw the line in the sand. It's only going to cause harm to your relationships. Instead, we're going to go through some actual language you can use to set boundaries. I will give you an example of what could work, and you will customize a script to better fit your specific financial situation and friendship dynamics.

EXERCISE
CREATING SCRIPTS TO SET BOUNDARIES

Counteroffer

When your friend asks you to come to happy hour, take a trip, get dinner, be in a wedding, or have a spa day and you want, or need, to say no, there's a special technique to make the entire exchange palatable for both parties. You can combine the counteroffer with the compliment sandwich because you sandwich the bad news in between a compliment or a thanks and then close it with a kind word + counteroffer.

Compliment/Thanks: "I really appreciate the invitation . . ."

Bad News: "But I'm focused on paying off my student loans by the end of this year." Or "It's a little out of my budget."

Kind Word + Counteroffer: "I definitely do want to spend time with you, though. Would you want to come over for game night instead?"

Think about one or two recent invites to which you wish you'd tried the counteroffer (or your bank account wishes you did). What would you say next time?

Compliment/Thanks

_____ .

_____ .

Bad News

_____ .

_____ .

Kind Word + Counteroffer

_____ .

_____ .

Share Your Reason

Being honest about the existence of debt or a high-level overview of your financial situation can help set a boundary for you. You don't have to share specifics if you aren't comfortable, but even stating, "I have student loan debt" or "I'm paying off credit card debt" or "We're trying to save up to buy a house" can provide context for your friends that they may not have had before. You shouldn't assume that people know what you have going on. In their mind, you just keep saying no every time they ask you to do something and they're worrying that you don't want to be their friend.

What financial goals or situations are you comfortable sharing with your friends? (It's okay to have different answers for different friends.)

_____

_____

_____

_____

How much detail are you comfortable sharing?

_____

_____

Take Control in Order to Manage Expectations

Being the self-appointed party planning committee helps, since making the social decisions in your friend group enables you to stay within your budget. But that sounds like a friend dictatorship, and that isn't conducive to a healthy relationship. Instead, you can directly set expectations.

"Could we pick a dinner spot that's no more than $20 each? I actually have a few ideas."

"I'd like to come out tonight, but I'm probably going to have only one drink because I'm on a budget."

Reflect on an upcoming invite (or one you're anticipating). How could you try taking control to manage expectations?

_____.

_____.

_____.

_____.

Can't Afford to Split the Bill

Group dinners were invented to test your ability to set boundaries. Splitting the bill evenly is the smoothest way to handle a group dinner, but it's not the most fair and equitable.

You're going to have to advocate for yourself and have the potentially awkward conversation. But I'm willing to bet at least one other person at that table will be relieved and will leap at the chance to just pay for what they ordered. Here is your formula:

(Counteroffer strategy) + (managing expectations) + (sharing your excuse) = the ideal way to navigate the splitting-the-dinner-bill conversation

Reduce the day-of tension by setting those expectations early and giving a ballpark range of your budget.

"I'm excited to catch up with everyone, but I'm really aiming to make a $500 payment toward my student loans this month, so I have to be mindful of my budget. Could we aim for a restaurant that won't cost more than $35 per person?"

Think about a recent or an upcoming group dinner and write down what you would say to provide context about your boundary and state your ballpark budget. And don't hesitate to send through some restaurant recommendations. Fast-casual, cafeteria-style restaurants where you order and pay individually and then sit down can really help reduce this tension!

_____.

_____.

_____.

Granted, it's not entirely fair to ask your friend to restrict options to what's in your budget, or if she's already made the selection because it's a special event. But you can also come in with the counteroffer.

"The restaurant you picked for your birthday dinner is delicious, but a little out of my budget. I really do still want to celebrate with you, so I'll just come for dessert or an after-dinner drink if that's okay."

What counteroffer could you have provided in a recent situation or will you use for an upcoming invite?

_____.

_____.

_____.

If none of this sounds good, you can also be the person that offers to split up the bill fairly (instead of evenly) at the end of the night. Another option is to try to speak to the waiter before the bill comes out and ask if your order (and itemize your order to the waiter) can be split off from the group? I saw this play out at a birthday dinner at which the woman I was seated next to pulled the waitress aside and said, "I didn't order any drinks, so would it be okay if I got the check for my entrée separately?" It wasn't an issue and she didn't have to deal with the rest of us splitting the bill evenly.

Helpful Hint: This strategy can also be used for other group social situations like a bachelorette party or bridal shower.

Don't Let Your Friend Keep Picking Up the Tab

As we age, life choices and careers can create an imbalance in who earns or has more to spend. It's possible a friend of yours could start to feel self-conscious about how much he or she has, which can lead to your friend offering to pay. At first, you might take her up on the offer—after all, she's making so much and can totally afford this. And she wouldn't offer if she didn't want to pay, right? Be wary of these situations. It's possible your friend will start to feel as if you're taking advantage.

You should make it clear that you don't expect that your friend will always pay.

"I want to pay next time, but I can't afford this restaurant. Are you okay with us eating at a cheaper place?"

Or it might make you feel uncomfortable that your friend keeps offering to pay.

"I appreciate the kind gesture, but it doesn't feel good for me."

Are there moments when someone has picked up a bill for you and you didn't know how to handle the situation?

_____.

_____.

_____.

Be Vulnerable with Your Friends

Being vulnerable with a friend takes a lot of trust and love, but sharing your truth also prevents your friend from thinking the worst. If one of your closest friends told you she couldn't come to your wedding because of work, that would be hurtful. But if she said, "I have six-figure student loan debt and just can't afford an international plane ticket," that is completely understandable. You might still be sad, but at least you would understand the why.

Sharing your financial vulnerabilities may also illuminate which friendships are meant to be lifelong bonds and which ones will undergo the natural phaseout. If a friend is throwing a hissy fit that you can't afford an international plane ticket, well, maybe she's not such a solid pal.

How to Decline an Invitation

No matter how well you set up a counteroffer strategy or share your specific situation, there are times your friends might still opt into something that's outside of your budget.

Whether you're trying to say no to a college friend reunion or attending a baby shower, one of the key moves is to decline sooner rather than later. Don't be the person who backs out at the last minute, especially if other people are depending on you to financially contribute.

"Sorry I can't come on the reunion trip, but I'd love to join digitally for a group happy hour one of the nights you're all there."

Or

"I'd love to take you out to dinner to celebrate your new adventure."

What are some ways you would decline a social invitation with a counteroffer?

_____.

_____.

_____.

You can also send a small gift as a token to offset any sting of declining, especially if it's a close friend. For example, one of my favorite baby shower moves is to send a book I loved to read as a kid (with a note explaining that) and a small gift for Mom, like nice bath salts or lotion.

While it's perfectly understandable to bow out of the financial obligations attached to certain functions, you do always want to be careful to strike a balance so that you're also investing in your relationships.

FOR WHEN YOU WANT TO JUST BE ABLE TO SAY YES

Perhaps boundaries are your thing. You excel at saying no and never feel peer-pressured into social situations that cost money. Whether that's you or not, there is one thing to consider: **If you say no enough times, people stop asking.** One of my big regrets from my early twenties was failing to invest in certain friendships because I was hyperfixated on my financial situation. I didn't want to spend money on most social engagements and always opted to pick up an extra shift over going out with friends.

EXERCISE
"FUN FUND" OR "FRIENDSHIP FUND" SAVINGS GOAL

Set aside money each month to put into a "Friend Fund" and give yourself permission, especially if you're in aggressive debt payoff or savings mode, to invest in time with your friends. Go to happy hour or movies, get a coffee, grab dinner, or just have some extra money to host friends for dinner at your place!

This is also a useful fund for those moments when your spending values aren't necessarily in alignment with a friend's. Sometimes you need to compromise and engage in what your friend wants to do, especially if it's important to them or a way to show support. This makes me flash back to all those nights of attending bad improv and sketch comedy shows! But I know that not all my friends want to come to personal finance events—and yet they will to support me.

Track Your Progress

Each money bag represents:

$ _____ toward my goal of $ _____.

Color in the money bags each time you make progress toward your goal.

EXERCISE
SETTING FINANCIAL BOUNDARIES WITH FRIENDS

Read through the checklist below and write down dates or particular situations for when you want to accomplish these goals.

❏ **Budget for looming expenses:** There are certain financial obligations for which you can prepare. Christmas comes the same time every year, and wedding season will eventually wallop you over the head. So start a savings account specifically for these kinds of pop-up but pricey moments in life so they don't blow your regular budget. _____/_____/20_____

_____.

_____.

❏ **Be honest:** Try the compliment sandwich to negotiate your friend's expensive suggestion to one that's within your own budget. _____/_____/20_____

_____.

_____.

❏ **Stand up for yourself, politely:** Let your friends in on your expectations and/or budget restrictions, but you can't be resentful if they still choose to partake. _____/_____/20_____

_____.

_____.

❏ **Don't be a financial foe:** Pay what you owe and/or be willing to negotiate if your buddy needs a cheaper alternative when hanging out. ____/_____/20_____

_____.

_____.

- -

GET YOUR FINANCIAL LIFE TOGETHER CHECK-IN

What is your biggest takeaway (or aha moment) from this chapter?

_____.

_____.

_____.

What feels the most overwhelming about this chapter?

_____.

_____.

_____.

Why does it feel so overwhelming to you in this moment?

_____.

_____.

_____.

Based on what you just learned, write down one actionable step you can take this week to improve your financial life.

_____.

_____.

_____.

Chapter 12

Getting Financially Naked with Your Partner

PEACH AND I casually chatted about money early on in our relationship. We'd routinely talk about vague topics like how much we felt comfortable spending on Christmas presents or what sounded like a good budget for a special date night or when we'd go Dutch versus when one of us would just pick up the tab. These smaller conversations eventually progressed to the bigger-picture discussions, which is how I discovered Peach had student loans. But it wasn't until we realized marriage could be a serious possibility that I asked him to share his number.

Chalk it up to my type A personality, but I wasn't willing to discuss an engagement, let alone a marriage, without knowing the financial situation in which I'd find myself after the "I do's." And neither should you.

Getting married (or otherwise committing to a lifelong partnership) is the biggest financial decision you'll make. And no, I don't mean the cost of a wedding. The actual commitment to another person. Marriage is fundamentally a decision to legally and financially bind yourself to another person. Sure, that strips away the romance and the love—but it's incredibly important to acknowledge. Money causes *a lot* of fights and tensions in relationships. Failure to communicate effectively about money with your partner is essentially dooming yourself to a series of the same fights over and over at the very least, or a costly separation or divorce.

Sorry, I know it's a heavy way to start this chapter.

In this chapter, you're going to learn how to start and navigate the almighty money talk with your partner. It might start with just shedding a few layers, but eventually, you will aim to achieve full-frontal financial nudity!

WHEN YOU SHOULD START TALKING ABOUT MONEY

(Because should you really be having that conversation before things are serious?)

The answer is: the earlier, the better. But I'm also a realist about how uncomfortable this conversation is for many people, and I understand that you might find yourself about to marry someone without ever directly discussing money. Luckily, the conversation is already happening without words.

EXERCISE
PICKING UP ON CONTEXT CLUES

How would you describe your lifestyle?

_____

_____

How would you describe your partner's lifestyle?

_____

_____

What did you do for your first date?

_____

_____

What types of dates do you go on now?

_____.

_____.

_____.

How do you decide who pays for certain activities or bills in the relationship?

_____.

_____.

_____.

What kinds of gifts do you give each other?

_____.

_____.

_____.

Have you vacationed together? Where did you go? Where did you stay? How did you get there? Who paid for what?

_____ .

_____ .

_____ .

_____ .

Your answers to these questions provide valuable insights into both your partner's financial situation and the emotional relationship you each have with money. The way you and your partner behave with money is evident in how you spend on bigger moments and day-to-day.

But context clues aren't enough. You need to have direct financial conversations with your partner.

HOW TO START TALKING ABOUT MONEY

You should never blindside your partner with this conversation. He or she may be reluctant to open this door, but you need to tell him or her it's going to happen.

"I would like for us to sit down and talk about money. It's really important we share our financial goals and situations with each other. Maybe we could even talk a bit about our financial baggage. When would be a good time for you to set aside time to talk this week?"

How will you bring this up to your partner?

_____ .

_____ .

Write down the time, date, and location for your financial talk:

Time:

Date: _____/_____/20_____

Location:

Helpful Hint: In private is usually the best option. But it's okay to bundle this potentially uncomfortable activity with something you love. Order your favorite take-out or bake a dessert you both love or plan to watch a show together afterward.

EXERCISE
PREPARING FOR YOUR MONEY TALK

Before you two actually sit down together, you both should take time to reflect on what you're willing to share at this moment and what you want to know from each other.

What I Want to Know and Share
Encourage your partner to take a sheet of paper and also fill out the answers to these questions before you two sit down together.

What I want to know about _____'s financial life is:

_____.

_____.

_____.

_____.

_____.

_____.

What I'm comfortable sharing with _____ **about my financial life is:**

_____.

_____.

_____.

_____.

_____.

Eventually, all the information needs to be shared (hence full-frontal financial nudity). But since it's the first conversation, you may be comfortable only admitting to the existence of student loans or credit card debt but not sharing the number.

That's okay. Just keep in mind that you eventually need to progress to sharing the details with your partner. Maybe you provide a range to contextualize it a bit for your partner. "I have more than $5,000 in credit card debt, but less than $10,000." Or "I have more than $20,000 in student loans."

Ready Your Poker Face

Can you imagine how awful it would feel to get naked in front of someone for the first time and have him or her laugh at you or make a face? Same goes for sharing your finances. It can feel vulnerable to get completely open about money with someone else. You *must* come into this conversation with a strong poker face. Do not have a dramatic reaction if your partner tells you about a high debt number or a credit-crushing mistake. Doing so can immediately ruin your partner's trust in you, and it will make it difficult to continue the talk now—or ever.

EXERCISE
INITIATING THE MONEY TALK

Okay, so all that has simply been the prep work to have this conversation. The natural next question is: But how do you actually initiate the talk?!

Here are my two favorite techniques:

Option #1: Break the tension with the truth.

"I know this is sort of an awkward conversation, but I feel it's really important as we continue to build our life together. What do you think?"

Option #2: The goal-setting strategy

"What's a financial goal you want to achieve in the next five years?"

[Partner answers] "And what's standing in your way?"

The perk of the second technique is that you can hint at the debt conversation without actually saying the D-word. It also starts to give you some ideas about what your partner values and hopes to achieve in the short to medium term.

Write down how you think your partner would best respond to you starting this conversation.

_____ .

_____ .

How would you want someone to initiate this conversation with you?

_____ .

_____ .

EXERCISE
THE INVENTORY: WHAT YOU NEED TO DISCUSS AND ANSWER

Now that you have a plan for how to initiate the discussion, here is a list of what you ultimately need to know about and share with your partner. **Reminder: You don't have to get every single question answered during your very first talk. This may be an ongoing process.**

Feel free to bring page 215 with you to your conversation and fill it out together as you progress through your discussion.

Financial Goals

You might've already mentioned one at the start of this conversation, but take the time to share what you want to financially achieve in the short (1–3 years), medium (4–9 years), and long term (10+ years).

Your goals as individuals and a couple will ultimately be the bedrock of your financial plan. This may feel like one of the easier topics to discuss, but keep in mind that it's one of the most critical.

Feel free to draw images or make lists that represent your goals.

MY SHORT-TERM $ GOALS ARE:	MY PARTNER'S SHORT-TERM $ GOALS ARE:

MY MEDIUM-TERM $ GOALS ARE:	MY PARTNER'S MEDIUM-TERM $ GOALS ARE:

MY LONG-TERM $ GOALS ARE:	MY PARTNER'S LONG-TERM $ GOALS ARE:

Your Emotional Relationship with Money

This is one of the most important things to learn during the financially naked conversation. It's critical that you understand your partner's emotional relationship to money, because it can inform so much about his or her decision-making and reactions to financial situations.

When I think about money, I feel:

_____.

_____.

When my partner thinks about money, they feel:

_____.

_____.

It's critical you learn how to fight fairly when in disputes about money. Understanding your partner's trigger points when it comes to money is an important part of communicating effectively. For example, someone who grew up in a household where money was tight may find it hard to splurge, even if it's within their financial means. Or it could manifest as wanting to constantly purchase things because they weren't able to in their childhood.

MY MONEY TRIGGERS	MY PARTNER'S MONEY TRIGGERS

You can also refer back to exercises completed in chapter 2 and encourage your partner to complete them as well.

Income

How much do you earn monthly and annually?

YOU	PARTNER
Monthly: $_____	Monthly: $_____
Annually: $_____	Annually: $_____

Types of Debt

What types of debt do you have (e.g., credit card, student loans, auto loan)?

*YOU:*_____

*PARTNER:*_____

How Much Debt You're Carrying

Fill in the grid below with the total balances.

TYPE OF DEBT	YOURS	PARTNER'S
Credit card	$	$
Student loans	$	$
Auto loan	$	$
Mortgage	$	$
Personal loan	$	$
Other	$	$
TOTAL	$	$

Credit Reports and Scores

You could print them out and swap if you want! Or you can show each other your credit score and your history with credit.

My credit score is _____.

My partner's credit score is _____.

Helpful Hint: A low credit score or a lot of debt needn't be a deal breaker! This should prompt questions about what caused a low credit score or the high debt. Past behaviors aren't as much of a concern as current ones. Consistently missing payments should be a red flag. But a low credit score could be as simple as a doctor's bill they didn't even know about that ended up in collections. (That happens to millions of Americans.)

Savings and Investments

How much do you each have saved up and invested for the future?

This is also a good chance for you to check in on your retirement plan and other investments if that's not a regular practice for you.

SAVINGS & INVESTMENTS	YOURS	PARTNER'S
Savings	$	$
Retirement account(s)	$	$
Other investments	$	$
TOTAL	$	$

CREATING A GAME PLAN

Those living together, married, or otherwise combining financial lives in some way need to build a game plan for how to handle their money.

Are You a Team or Individuals?

Is it *your* money and *my* money or *our* money?

Now, my personal bias is that you shouldn't merge finances until after you're married. It has nothing to do with the depth or seriousness of your relationship and more to do with the legal implications. Marriage brings a certain protocol for how assets are divided up in a divorce. Breakups don't. Should you have a joint account with your partner, they are entitled to drain a joint bank account. Plus, if your partner creates debt that's charged to a joint account, there is a chance you could be held liable.

For married couples, the default is often joint finances—but that doesn't have to be the case. It is perfectly acceptable to stay separate.

There are three main camps when it comes to handling money in marriage: totally joint, totally separate, or a hybrid model of both.

There aren't right and wrong answers here. It's about what works best for the two of you from an emotional perspective as well as a practical one.

EXERCISE
QUESTIONS TO ANSWER WHEN CREATING A GAME PLAN

When you're developing your own game plan, you should discuss logistics like:

Who pays which bills? This will certainly change over time, especially if you decide to morph from cohabitating to married and banking jointly.

_____.

_____.

Where are your salaries going? Do you comingle them all into a joint account from which every bill is paid, or are you more of a multiple-bank-accounts kind of couple? You also need to decide how much of your income is going toward bills, savings, investments, debt repayment, and spending money.

_____ .

_____ .

What are your financial priorities? As you discuss your financial goals, you have to decide which ones you're prioritizing and which ones get less attention—or if they get completely benched for a time period.

_____ .

_____ .

OTHER IMPORTANT QUESTIONS TO ASK EACH OTHER ABOUT MONEY

As life changes and new financial situations unfold, you may find it's important to reevaluate how you and your partner handle money. Depending on your unique situation, here are some other questions you may want to (eventually) ask each other.

"Okay, for a long time our situations were similar and it worked to do 50/50, but now that our incomes aren't balanced, this situation doesn't feel equitable. How do you feel?"

"Even though we've been in a serious relationship for a while now, we do have different lifestyle expectations. What do you envision our lifestyle being like after we move in together/get married?"

"I'm comfortable paying more toward rent if you agree to pay $X amount more toward student loans/credit cards."

"How much should we each be able to spend without checking in with the other?"

"I love you, but we've been really struggling to communicate effectively about money. I feel like it's time to go speak to a professional. What do you think?"

If you're interested in how to navigate other critical financial conversations, then you should check out the third book in this series: *Broke Millennial Talks Money*.

- -

Get Your Financial Life Together Check-In

What is your biggest takeaway (or aha moment) from this chapter?

_____.

_____.

_____.

What feels the most overwhelming about this chapter?

_____.

_____.

_____.

Why does it feel so overwhelming to you in this moment?

_____.

_____.

_____.

Based on what you just learned, write down one actionable step you can take this week to improve your financial life.

_____.

_____.

_____.

Chapter 13

How to Negotiate Salary (or Anything Else) by Learning to Ask for What You Want

WE ARE OFTEN our own worst enemies when it comes to negotiating. Why? Because we love to avoid awkward conversations. The social dynamics of a workplace are filled with tense money conversations. Everything from asking a coworker how much they earn to negotiating with your boss for a raise to being honest that you can't afford to go out to lunch at that bougie new spot near the office.

Learning how to negotiate is often framed around your salary, and yes, that's important, but there are so many points in life that require negotiating. Plus, regular opportunities to practice the skill of negotiating in a low-stakes way prepare you for when it's really going to matter.

Whether you're negotiating with a landlord, your cell phone service provider, or your manager at work—it's a critical life skill that helps safeguard, and grow, the money in your bank account. It's okay if the thought of negotiating currently makes you queasy—but you can't allow it to stay that way. This is a necessary asset on your journey to get your financial life together.

INFORMATION IS POWER

"How much are you willing to pay to avoid an awkward conversation?"

Alexandra Dickinson, a negotiation expert, posed this question when I interviewed her for *Broke Millennial Talks Money*, and my expression might as well have embodied that mind-blown emoji.

It's such a simple question and truly at the heart of this entire topic.

But really, how much are you willing to pay to avoid an awkward conversation of any sort?

$_____

Now, sometimes you might put a price tag on an awkward conversation, and that's understandable. But it's important you understand the possible ramifications. Here is a completely true story of my own about why we need to talk numbers.

Years ago, I was hired to be part of a panel discussion that required me to fly across the country. When asked how much I would charge, I said: "Um, $3,000 plus travel expenses?" I even phrased my response as a question.

"Oh, yeah, that works great for us," said the woman hiring.

A friend of mine was hired to speak on the same panel. We had similar experience levels. We were both traveling from the same city to this speaking engagement. We were both women and nearly the same age. It was as if all the possible factors for why we'd get paid different amounts had been deliberately controlled for in this particular case just to teach me a lesson.

Over dinner, and after a little liquid courage, I directly asked my friend how much she was getting paid for speaking on the panel. "$10,000," she told me.

My jaw dropped. She was making $7,000 more than I was for the same work! While a little bit of envy crept into my brain, I was mostly so appreciative that she shared that information because it showed me what was possible.

This could sound like a hyperbolic example, especially if you aren't self-employed. But small discrepancies in pay can have long-term wealth-building implications, especially when you factor in investing for retirement.

Now it's time for you to learn how to ask, "How much do you make?"

Did You Know: In the United States, it is illegal under the National Labor Relations Act[1] for most employers to bar their employees from discussing salaries, and it's illegal to fire them for doing so. You still need to proceed with caution before gabbing about salaries without any potential consequences. You really need to know your office climate and whether your employer tries (possibly illegally) to prevent these conversations from happening. It may be illegal to fire you for striking up conversations about salaries, but that doesn't mean it's illegal to find another cause to justify giving you the ax.

EXERCISE
GETTING THE INFO YOU NEED

Who Should I Ask?

Dickinson recommends asking three types of people:

1. Someone who does your role at your company or at a similar company

2. Someone who has been promoted out of your role recently

3. Somebody who hires for your role

Fill in the following table with the names of people you know who fall into the categories.

Keep in mind that you want a spectrum of people in each category (e.g., don't ask just men or just women).

SAME ROLE AS MINE AT MY COMPANY	SIMILAR ROLE TO MINE AT A SIMILAR COMPANY	RECENTLY PROMOTED OUT OF MY ROLE	HIRING MANAGER FOR MY ROLE

What to Say

Dickinson has a three-sentence script to get through the potential awkwardness of bluntly asking someone how much he or she makes.

Sentence 1: "I'm doing research because . . . [insert your reason]."

For example, the reason could be asking for a raise or trying to determine if your salary is within range or interviewing for a new position.

Sentence 2: "And I think you have some information that could help me."

Sentence 3: "Would you be willing to share your ballpark salary with me?"

Alternatively, if you're asking someone who hires for your role or is a mentor or a former boss or just generally in a higher position in the company, then Dickinson recommends amending the third line to "I'm thinking of asking for $X. Does that sound reasonable to you?"

Customize your own script:

I'm doing research because _____.

And I think you have information that could help me.

Would you be willing to share your ballpark salary with me?

or

I'm thinking of asking for $_____. Does that sound reasonable to you?

Another option is to use the over/under strategy.

I'm doing research because _____.

Do you make over or under $_____?

or

Is it appropriate for me to ask for over or under $_____ for this [job/raise]?

You can keep following up with the over/under strategy. For example, if you're asking, "Do you make over or under $50,000?" and the person says, "Over," you can ask, "Over or under $55,000?" until you get closer to the range that's helpful.

WAIT, I REALLY DON'T FEEL COMFORTABLE ASKING MY COWORKERS (OR I WORK FOR A SMALL COMPANY)

You may not have the luxury of feeling safe enough to ask coworkers how much they make or perhaps you work for a small company. Don't stress! There is an alternative option for you.

EXERCISE
POWER OF THE COLD PITCH

The digital age has given us a multitude of ways to make connections. Instead of asking coworkers directly, you could take your question to the Internet. Well, in a tactful way. Cold-pitching people on LinkedIn who fall into the categories from the "Getting the Info You Need" exercise or your college's alumni network can give you access to more data points.

Fill in the Blanks

Hi, I'm a _____ *[job title] and* _____

_____ *[reason for asking]. I'm preparing to ask for a raise (or for a job interview). In order to best prepare, it would be helpful if you could share what you believe is an appropriate salary for someone who does my job.*

Customize your own script to cold-pitch.

_____.

_____.

_____.

_____.

Tracking Your Cold Pitches
Keep track of everyone you've pitched by filling in the table on the next page.

NAME	TITLE	DATE PITCHED

Helpful Hint: Asking how much someone else charges is incredibly important for freelancers/contractors/the self-employed. It may feel awkward at first, but these conversations could put, quite literally, thousands to tens of thousands of dollars into your bank account over the long run.

GETTING READY TO NEGOTIATE

You've gathered information and now you're ready to actually negotiate. A common mistake is waiting too long to actually make the ask. For example, if you know raises are typically given during your annual review, you shouldn't be asking for a raise at your annual review. Sounds strange? Well, companies generally set their budgets in advance of when raises (or bonuses) are distributed. If you wait until you're being told about a raise or bonus, then a budget has likely already been set. Instead, you should talk to your manager three to four months prior.

One way to set an expectation that you'd like to receive a raise or promotion is to state it plainly while asking for a road map about how to get there.

I'd like to discuss what I can do to move up to [insert position here] _____

_____ or to increase my salary to $_____. Any constructive criticism

or recommendations on skills to build or improve on would be really appreciated.

EXERCISE
SUCCESS TRACKER

Whether you're traditionally or self-employed, it's helpful to keep track of ways your contributions to the company or performances for clients have been successful.

I personally like to utilize a system called "the success folder." It's not a particularly clever or unique name, but it works. This is a folder I keep on my computer and use to track triumphs as they unfold so I'm not scouring my inbox or trying to recall victories months (or even a year+) later.

Examples of what to put in your own success folder include:

- Metrics proving you performed better on a project than anticipated

- Proof of personal growth in your position over the year

- Picking up new responsibilities

- Doing tasks that are above your designated title to prove you're ready for a promotion

- Praise from clients, managers, or coworkers

Take a moment to brainstorm some success-folder-worthy moments you've had in recent months:

_____.

_____.

_____ .

_____ .

_____ .

_____ .

MAKING THE BIG ASK

EXERCISE
FILL IN THE BLANKS

"One of my all-time favorite lines is 'I would like,'" says Alexandra Dickinson. "It's not 'I want,' 'I need,' 'I deserve,' and it's not 'I was wondering . . .'" It's not demanding or wishy-washy; it's right down the middle."

What is your answer to "I would like"?

I would like _____ .

_____ .

Now try a more direct approach with additional context.

In my market research, I found that the top performers in this field make $_____ .

I consider myself a top performer based on _____

_____ .

I would like $_____ or as close as possible to it.

Or when negotiating in a job interview:

Based on market rates and my skill set, my desired salary for this position is $_____.

But what if you work for a small business or you know that raises aren't going to be large this year? If you decide you want to stay with that company for other reasons (work-life balance, workplace culture, learning opportunities, etc.), then you could try to negotiate for more than salary.

It's really important to me to raise my salary. I think something like $_____ would be more in line with the market, but if you can't do that, it would be a great benefit to me to be able to [insert request here] _____.

Here are common things for which you can negotiate outside of salary:

- Vacation time

- Working remotely

- Flextime, especially if you need to come in later or leave earlier one day a week to pick up or drop off a child

- More funds for professional development or education

- An intern

- More time off for parental leave

- Leadership opportunities

EXERCISE
PRACTICE AWKWARD SILENCE

The next time you're on the phone or a Zoom meeting or just talking to a friend in person, try going silent for five seconds. Seriously. A full five I'm-counting-with-Mississippis seconds. Just see what the other person does. We are often so uncomfortable in silence, that we try to fill the void. This is a powerful tool in negotiation.

I've done my research and according to what I've found the market rate for this kind of role is $_____, and for all the reasons that we've discussed about my performance and contributions, I'd like a raise of ___ percent.

And then just shut up!

You need to practice feeling comfortable in silence *before* you get into a negotiation so it's less awkward for you to let it hang after you make the direct ask.

Write down three low-stakes ways you can practice asking for something and letting the silence hang. Try to get a little creative! It can even be as low stakes as asking your friend/sibling/partner/roommate to watch a show with you they normally wouldn't.

I would like you to watch Real Housewives *with me tonight. (SILENCE)*

_____ .

_____ .

_____ .

WHAT IF YOU GET A NO?

There are a few factors to consider here depending on the type of negotiation.

If you leveraged another offer to try to get your current employer to give you a raise, then you might need to walk and take the new offer. Leveraging another offer and then staying could lessen your leverage in the future. It may also sully the dynamic at work, depending on your workplace relationships.

If you tried to negotiate for a raise at your current job with no leverage, then you could simply ask: "Can you give me a sense of what it would take to earn that raise?" Go back to the concept of asking for constructive criticism, which provides a road map. If your manager can't seem to give you helpful feedback, then it might be time to spruce up the résumé and start looking for another job.

If you get a no to a salary negotiation in a job interview process but still want to take the new position, you can say:

"I really appreciate you considering it, but I'm excited about the job and I'd love to accept regardless."

EXERCISE
PRACTICE LOW-STAKES NEGOTIATIONS THIS WEEK

This is one skill that you cannot improve upon without human interaction. Your challenge is to practice at least two negotiating strategies in your daily life within the next week.
Suggestions:

I would like. Get comfortable with the language "I would like" by using it in your everyday life. It could be with a coworker ("I would like you to get me that data by the end of the day") or a partner ("I would like you to handle the grocery shopping this week") or anyone else!

Ask for a deal at a store. Here's a really simple strategy. Go to a café close to closing time and ask if you can get a pastry for free with your drink. After all, they'll probably throw out whatever's left anyway.

Let silence hang. Whether it's with roommates or coworkers or the person with whom you try to negotiate at the store—you need to make your ask and then let it hang for at least five seconds without you following up.

Bonus challenge. Directly ask a coworker how much he or she earns using the over/under strategy.

Write down what your low-stakes negotiations were and how they went:

_____.

_____.

_____.

_____.

_____.

Get Your Financial Life Together Check-In

What is your biggest takeaway (or aha moment) from this chapter?

_____.

_____.

_____.

What feels most overwhelming about this chapter?

_____.

_____.

_____.

Why does it feel so overwhelming to you in this moment?

_____.

_____.

_____.

Based on what you just learned, write down one actionable step you can take this week to improve your financial life.

_____.

_____.

_____.

Chapter 14

Investing: No, It Isn't Gambling!
(In Fact, You've Probably Already Started.)

"I'M NOT READY to invest" is still far too common a refrain, especially as the millennial population ages into our forties! Investing is one of the most effective ways you can build wealth. It takes consistent action, a dash of fortitude, and patience. You don't have to be skilled at picking the latest hottest stock (in fact, you definitely shouldn't). You don't have to hop on the newest trend (e.g., crypto and NFTs). You just need to understand a few basics and be consistent.

It's time to remove the fear and unpack the misconceptions about what it means to be an investor, because it isn't just for the wealthy.

UNDERSTANDING THE BEAUTY OF COMPOUND INTEREST

The basic way to explain compound interest is that it's your interest earning interest.

For example, if you invest $100 and get an 8 percent return after year one, you have $108. You decide not to invest anything else and to just leave the $108 alone. In year two, you would be earning interest not only on your initial $100 investment, but on the additional $8, so the full $108. If you get another 8 percent return, you've earned $8.64 and now have $116.64.

You might have experienced the wrath of compound interest working against you when you have debt. It's the reason it feels like the principal balance on your credit card or student loans just never seems to go down. That same horrible effect can be harnessed for good when you invest.

Try playing around with one of my favorite compound interest calculators from the SEC on an official government website at www.investor.gov/financial-tools-calculators/calculators /compound-interest-calculator.

EXERCISE
COMPOUND INTEREST

Use the compound interest calculator to find the expected future balance of your investment. I recommend just leaving the compound frequency at annually.

INITIAL INVESTMENT	MONTHLY CONTRIBUTION	LENGTH OF TIME IN YEARS	ESTIMATED INTEREST RATE	TOTAL
$1,000	$150	15	8%	$
$1,000	$150	45	8%	$
$0	$250	35	10%	$
$0	$250	40	10%	$
$5,000	$0	30	8%	$
$5,000	$0	40	8%	$
$3,000	$500	45	7%	$
$3,000	$500	45	9%	$

This table shows what happens if you just save your money and helps you better understand the impact of compound interest, the importance of consistent monthly contributions, and the significance of five or ten years when the magic fairy dust of compound interest is sprinkled upon your money.

INITIAL INVESTMENT	MONTHLY CONTRIBUTION	LENGTH OF TIME IN YEARS	TOTAL IF YOU ONLY SAVED
$1,000	$150	15	$28,000
$1,000	$150	45	$82,000
$0	$250	35	$105,000
$0	$250	40	$120,000
$5,000	$0	30	$5,000*
$5,000	$0	40	$5,000*
$3,000	$500	45	$273,000

Give or take a little bit depending on savings account interest rates. If the savings account offered 0.50%, then it would probably be around $5,800 in savings after 30 years and $6,100 after 40 years.

DECODING JARGON

One of the most frustrating parts about investing is learning the language. It's intimidating at first. But that's okay. It's no different from learning terminology for any artistic pursuit or sport or job. It's important to take the time to start learning investing concepts and terms.

EXERCISE
MATCH THE TERMS

GENERAL INVESTING TERMS

Match the definition in the right-hand column with the term in the left-hand column. You can find the answer key on page 273.

1. Compound interest _____	a. Fancy way of asking "How long until you need to use the money you're investing?"
2. Diversification _____	b. These words are often used interchangeably. Equities and stocks are synonyms meaning you own a piece of a company. Shares are what your stock is divided into. Stocks are the pizza. Shares are the slices.
3. Time Horizon _____	c. A hybrid option between mutual fund investing and just buying/selling stocks because you can trade instantly during the day. Mutual fund transactions occur at the end of the day instead of in real time.
4. Risk Tolerance _____	d. Fee you pay to help cover operational costs the brokerage incurs. 0.62% means you'll pay $6.20 for every $1,000 invested. This is critical. Lower the fee = more money you keep invested and growing for the future.
5. Asset Class _____	e. A payment you get from the company or fund in which you invested for being a shareholder. These are a result of earnings.
6. Asset Allocation _____	f. Industries like health care, energy, tech, and real estate. Buying a share of Apple means you own a single stock in a single sector (tech).
7. Brokerage _____	g. Gut reaction you feel about losing money (and you may need to learn how to combat your natural reaction).
8. Equities/stocks/shares _____	h. The magic reason consistent small investments grow into a big nest egg. In short, you earn interest on your interest, which helps create a snowball effect.
9. Sectors _____	i. Making sure the asset classes in which you invest align with your goals, risk tolerance, and time horizon. 70/30 could mean 70% stocks and 30% bonds.

10. Bonds _____	**j.** Your money gets pooled with other investors to buy hundreds to thousands of stocks or bonds that are bundled into the fund. Way less shady than it sounds. (Actively managed, meaning a professional builds the portfolio.)
11. Index _____	**k.** The company that buys and sells investments on your behalf.
12. Mutual Fund _____	**l.** The investing version of "Don't put all your eggs in one basket." You don't want to invest in just a single asset class or a single stock or sector.
13. Index Fund _____	**m.** Technically a type of mutual fund, but no professional is involved and it just mirrors an index. Usually has a lower expense ratio than a mutual fund.
14. ETF (aka Exchange Traded Fund) _____	**n.** A grouping of similar investments. IPA, lager, ale, and stout are all beer. Beer would be the asset class with IPA, lager, ale, and stout being the similar investments.
15. Expense Ratio _____	**o.** You own a piece of a corporation's debt or government's debt when you buy one of these. Generally considered a less risky investment.
16. Dividend _____	**p.** A way to measure the market's performance by looking at a statistically significant portion, like the S&P 500, which is an index of stocks issued by 500 large publicly traded companies.

Pop Quiz: Are You an Investor?

Circle which answer describes you.

1. Do you have access to a retirement account through work, such as a 401(k), IRA, or 403(b)?

   Yes / No

2. If you're self-employed, are you contributing to a retirement account such as an IRA, SEP IRA, SIMPLE IRA, Solo 401(k)?

   Yes / No

3. Are the funds you contribute to those accounts invested or sitting in cash?

Invested / Sitting in Cash

Helpful Hint: Not sure if your money is invested? Here are some things to look for:

1. Where is your money sitting? If the fund has the words "cash" or "settlement" in the name, then it's not invested.

2. Has your retirement account grown much in the last few years? If it's only marginally different from the amount you put in, then it's probably sitting in cash. (Granted, this assumes the stock market is performing well.)

3. You can always call and ask customer service! Explain that you're just learning about investing and you're a little unclear whether the money in your retirement account is actually invested or is just sitting in cash, waiting for you to pick investments. There is zero shame in this. You have no idea how many folks experience this exact situation on their investing journey.

4. Do you have any money outside of retirement accounts invested in the stock market?

Yes / No

If your answers were "Yes" to questions one or two, "Invested" to question three, or just "Yes" to question four, then guess what? You're an investor!

It's incredibly common for people to not consider themselves investors, even when they're investing in their retirement accounts. I believe this could be because we use the wrong language when we talk about retirement.

YOU'RE NOT SAVING FOR RETIREMENT, YOU'RE *INVESTING* FOR RETIREMENT

The language we use matters, and financial professionals and educators do everyone a disservice by continuing to say "save for retirement." I understand it sounds and feels more accessible to people, but it's not accurate. **You aren't saving for retirement. You're *investing* for retirement.**

Stressed about how to pick the investments in your retirement account? An easy starter option is called a Target Date Fund (sometimes a life cycle fund or all-in-one fund). It's tied to an approximate year you'd retire, like 2065, and ensures your money is invested with a risk profile that's reasonable for your age. There are pros and cons, with a con being that it's a one-size-fits-all solution when your investments should be tailored to you and your goals. But a big pro is that it makes sure your money is invested, which is the most important thing, and you can always change to different investments in the future.

WHY INVESTING FOR YOUR FUTURE IS IMPORTANT

Flip back to chapter 3 and reread your answer for the Dream Retirement exercise on page 31.

Write down some of those dreams here.

_____ .

_____ .

_____ .

_____ .

The dreams you just wrote down are why it's important to invest for your future. It's not important because I'm saying it is or your parents say so or that angry guy on that business show your dad likes to watch in the morning yells about it. It's because investing for your long-term future is one of the most effective ways to reach your goals.

Think about it this way.

Jodi wants $1,000,000 as her retirement nest egg. If she invested $325 a month for 40 years (e.g., 25 years old to 65 years old) and received an average 8% return on her investments, then she'd have about $1,010,000.

If Jodi didn't want to invest and just wanted to save the money, she would need to save about $2,000 per month for 40 years to achieve the same goal.

Compound interest puts in a lot of the work when you're investing in a way that saving alone just doesn't do.

EXERCISE
RETIREMENT GOAL SETTING

You've taken some time to reflect on your dream retirement. You've considered some of the costs you'll need to contend with in retirement. You've checked out recommended benchmarks. Now you need to set a goal for yourself.

It's probably still not clear how much you'll need exactly because there are so many unknown variables. But truly think about how much you need each month to live your desired (but realistic) lifestyle. Would $5,000 a month cover your basic needs plus some extras? What about $10,000? Definitely add some cushion because, you know, inflation.

My monthly budget for a nice life in retirement will be $_____.

($_____) × 12 = $_____ will be your annual spend

($_____ annual spend) × 25 = $_____ how much you need to retire

Multiply by 25 Rule: The Multiply by 25 Rule is a calculation based on the assumption that your retirement will last thirty years and that you're using the 4 Percent Rule—which is addressed in the next exercise.

If I determined it would cost $10,000 a month to live my desired retirement, then I would need $120,000 in annual spend. $120,000 × 25 = $3 million is my retirement goal.

Ready to put that number to the test?

EXERCISE
TESTING THAT RETIREMENT GOAL

One of the most popular retirement rules of thumb is the 4 Percent Rule.

4 Percent Rule: If you withdraw 4 percent or less of your portfolio per year and have an appropriate mix of stocks and bonds for your current risk tolerance and phase of life, then your money should last you at least 30 years.

A $1 million retirement nest egg sounds like a lot of money as a lump sum, but when the 4 percent rule is applied, it means $40,000 per year. $1,000,000 × 0.04% = $40,000.

The 4 Percent Rule is based on the 1998 Trinity Study. Even the eldest of millennials were still under 18 when that study was performed, which should make us question if it's still applicable. To err on the side of caution, you can use 2 or 3 percent instead of 4 percent when running your own calculations.

Try using it yourself!

Your retirement account goal $_____ × 0.04 = $_____

That's how much you'd have to spend annually and not run out for 30 years. You can adjust for a lower withdrawal rate.

Your retirement account goal $_____ × 0.03 = $_____

Your retirement account goal $_____ × 0.02 = $_____

Should you decide to be more conservative, which isn't a bad idea depending on how much wiggle room you need to feel secure, then the Multiply by 25 Rule won't be as effective.

DECODING JARGON, PART II

<table>
<tr><td colspan="2" align="center">EXERCISE
MATCH THE TERMS</td></tr>
</table>

RETIREMENT INVESTING TERMS

Match the definition in the right-hand column with the term in the left-hand column.

(Note that the table continues on the opposite page.) You can find the answers on page 274.

1. 401(k)/403(b)/IRA _____	a. When you get to keep your employer match if you leave your job. You always keep your contributions. There are three main types.
2. Roth _____	b. You put the money in pretax, which lowers your taxable income, meaning you probably pay less in taxes today. But you do have to pay taxes when you use the money in retirement.
3. Traditional _____	c. You can leave your job at any point and keep the employer match.
4. Employer Match _____	d. Your employer puts money into your retirement account, equaling your contribution up to a certain percentage.
5. Vesting Schedule _____	e. Not all the same, but all different types of retirement plans. 401(k)s and 403(b)s are usually offered by employers, but an IRA you can open yourself.
6. Immediate _____	f. An investment fund that is tied to an approximate year you'd retire, like 2065. It automatically starts your investments more aggressively when you're young and ages them to be more conservative as you get closer to retirement. A fine option for people who don't know which investments to pick when they first open up a retirement account.
7. Cliff _____	g. You put money into your retirement account after paying taxes. There is no tax advantage today, but you take the money out tax-free in retirement.

8. Graded _____	h. A cost you'll pay (in addition to taxes) if you take your money out of your retirement account before you're 59.5 years old. This is to discourage people from raiding retirement accounts. There are some loopholes, but be wary of taking money out.
9. Target date fund _____	i. You have to wait until your employer contribution "vests" to keep any of the match. This often happens around year five of employment. If you leave prior, you get to take only your contributions.
10. Early withdrawal penalty _____	j. Each year a percentage of your employer contribution vests until it reaches 100% (e.g., 0% in year 1, 20% in year 2, 40% in year 3 . . .).

INVESTING ISN'T JUST FOR THE WEALTHY

If there's one big takeaway from this chapter, well, I probably want it to be that you're investing for retirement—not saving! But if there's a second big takeaway, you should feel affirmed in the truth that investing isn't just for those who are already wealthy. You too can be an investor. Yes, even if you have student loans! At the very least, you should still be contributing to your retirement account enough to get the employer match or putting money in an IRA.

Ready to level up your investing game (or just learn more in preparation)? Check out *Broke Millennial Takes On Investing: A Beginner's Guide to Leveling Up Your Money*.

- -

Get Your Financial Life Together Check-In

What is your biggest takeaway (or aha moment) from this chapter?

_____.

_____.

_____.

What feels the most overwhelming about this chapter?

_____ .

_____ .

_____ .

Why does it feel so overwhelming to you in this moment?

_____ .

_____ .

_____ .

Based on what you just learned, write down one actionable step you can take this week to improve your financial life.

_____ .

_____ .

_____ .

Chapter 15

I'm Not Rich Enough to Hire a Financial Planner

I KNOW YOU'RE tempted, or downright planning, to just skip this chapter. After all, you're a broke (or just barely above-broke) millennial. The notion of paying someone to help you with your finances sounds ludicrous. Except maybe it isn't.

Gone are the days of financial planning being accessible only to silver-haired multimillionaires. Remember, investing isn't just for the wealthy and neither is financial planning. At the very least, you should do the "What Do I Want from a Financial Planner?" exercise before completely dismissing this chapter. That exercise will also help you further clarify your own pain points as you continue your financial journey.

You might even need some of the knowledge for later; you know, after you develop an app Google acquires or become a media darling, thanks to starring on the newest hit reality TV show, or your content creator work turns into a book deal. Hey, it can happen.

Before we get into the education piece around financial planning, you should take some time to reflect about what you'd want from a financial planner.

EXERCISE
WHAT DO I WANT FROM A FINANCIAL PLANNER?

Fill in the statements below as if you're getting ready to hire a financial planner. Don't fixate on whether or not you can afford one or if one would even take the time to meet with you based on your current financial situation. Just focus on preparing for the process.

I want a financial planner who will:

_____.

_____.

I want someone who understands:

_____.

_____.

I am most confused about:

_____.

_____.

I am most worried about:

_____.

_____.

It would make me feel better if my financial planner could:

_____ .

_____ .

I want my financial planner to specialize in:

_____ .

_____ .

I want my financial planner to have worked with clients who also:

_____ .

_____ .

WHAT EXACTLY DOES A FINANCIAL PLANNER DO?

A financial planner helps you get your financial house in order and can provide an objective, nonemotional third-party opinion about how to best grow and protect your wealth. This can be key during major life transitions like buying a home, getting married, having a baby, caring for a family member, inheriting money, or getting divorced.

IS IT FINANCIAL PLANNER OR FINANCIAL ADVISOR?
WHY DO I KEEP SEEING BOTH TERMS?

Frankly, it is just a little confusing. These terms can have different meanings, but they're also used interchangeably.

The simple way to differentiate is that a financial planner often has an area of expertise, i.e., investing or retirement planning, and may hold certain certifications. A financial advisor is more of an all-inclusive term and can refer to stockbrokers, insurance salesmen, estate planners, and all sorts of folks who sell, manage, or advise on a facet of your financial life.

Because financial advisors can sell products to you, it's important to be careful with your understanding of the relationship you're developing. Sometimes a person can use the term "financial advisor" to sound as if they are looking out for you when really they're motivated to sell to you and receive a commission. Don't worry. You're going to learn more about this.

FIDUCIARY VS. SUITABILITY: WHO IS REALLY LOOKING OUT FOR YOUR BEST INTERESTS?

Financial planners and advisors are both likely to recommend products to you. Those products might be insurance policies or investments or estate planning services. Because of this relationship, it's important that you work with a financial planner who is a fiduciary.

- *Fiduciary:* Recommends a product that's in your best interest and not necessarily in the best interest of a financial advisor (i.e., the product might not get the advisor the highest commission or even any commission!).

- *Suitability:* Recommends (or sells) you a product that's—as the name implies— suitable. It won't harm you, but it might not be what's best either.

Did You Know: You want the financial planner with whom you have an ongoing relationship and who is helping build your financial plan to be a fiduciary. However, it's quite possible you'll need insurance or other financial products prior to hiring a financial planner. The person selling you insurance (e.g., a life insurance policy) might not be a fiduciary and will probably have an excellent sales pitch. That's why you need to understand your needs and the product that makes the most sense for you before you get on the phone and hear that sales pitch.

There is no legal obligation for any financial planner to be held to the fiduciary standard, unless you have a signed oath that he or she will do so.

Writing things down helps to get it to stick in your memory. So I want you to write down what it means to be a fiduciary.

I want my financial planner to be a fiduciary because a fiduciary is someone who:

_____ .

Certain firms or financial planner networks may require all of its members to be held to the fiduciary standard. Notably, certified financial planners are bound to this oath as part of becoming CFPs.

HOW DOES YOUR FINANCIAL ADVISOR OR PLANNER GET PAID?

Fiduciary versus suitability is relevant because of how the payment structures work within the financial planning industry. There are three main ways your financial planner (or advisor) gets paid:

1. Commission

2. Fee-only

3. Fee and Commission (sometimes called Fee-based)

Commission: Obviously, if a person is working based on earning that sweet, sweet commish, then he's probably more likely to slot you into whatever product puts the most dough in his pocket, just as long as it's suitable for you. Now, if held to the fiduciary standard, it would need to be the best possible product for you, regardless of commission rates.

Fee-only: Working exactly as the term sounds, the fee-only advisors, as defined by the CFP Board, never take commission for any advice they give. There's even an additional level of strictness that dictates advisors cannot even put themselves in a position to possibly accept commission at some point. You pay fee-only advisors a flat-rate fee for their services.

Fee-based: This does blur the lines between the strict fee-only and the suitability-focused commission advisors. These advisors sound legit up front because the planning is fee-based, but they can earn a commission on recommended products (e.g., an insurance policy). To add in another layer of confusion, their financial advice can be fiduciary while their product recommendations could be suitability, but they are supposed to disclose to you whether they receive commission on a recommended product. Does your brain hurt yet?

Fee-only simplifies your relationship with a financial advisor.

BEFORE YOU HIRE a financial planner, you need to do some reflecting about what you want. You guessed it. We're going back to goal setting! Your goals will be the basis of your financial plan and it's something you need to be able to communicate effectively to your financial planner.

EXERCISE
SHARING MY GOALS

Here's where I am now and where I'd like to be in the next year:

_____.

_____.

_____.

_____.

The financial anxieties keeping me up at night are:

_____.

_____.

_____.

_____.

My ultimate financial dream is to have enough money to:

_____.

_____.

_____.

_____.

My top three financial concerns in the next five years are:

_____.

_____.

_____.

_____.

GETTING READY TO HIRE YOUR OWN FINANCIAL PLANNER

At this point, how do you feel about finding and hiring a financial planner?

_____.

_____.

It's okay if you wrote down words like "overwhelmed," "stressed," or "anxious."

You want to find the right ethical person to help you handle your money and it can feel like there are a lot of potential traps out there.

Despite the unregulated nature of the financial planning industry, it's actually not too difficult to vet a potential financial planner.

You can start by going straight for the gold standard: a Certified Financial Planner™.

A CFP® designation means the person has gone through a rigorous program with strict regulations under the oversight of the CFP Board. CFPs must also adhere to the fiduciary standards as well as the CFP Board's ethics and standards.

You don't *have* to use a CFP as your financial advisor, but doing so should help you get the best value for your money.

EXERCISE
CHECKLIST: PREPARING TO HIRE A FINANCIAL PLANNER

Check the boxes that apply.

Does your financial planner have a clean record?

❏ Yes

❏ No

Go to brokercheck.finra.org and type in your planner's name.

You can also check cfp.net/verify-a-cfp-professional and adviserinfo.sec.gov.

You will see details about their license (e.g., which exams they've passed), work history, disclosure or ethics violations, and state license. This can help you verify if what your financial planner is telling you is legit. Want to give it a test run? Put in the name "Bernard Madoff."

How does your financial planner get paid?

❏ Commission

❏ Fee-only

❏ Fee & Commission (aka Fee-based)

Not sure? Just ask, "How do you get paid?" If you're receiving free advice, then it's very likely the advisor is getting paid via commission for selling you products.

Is your financial planner a fiduciary?

❏ Yes

❏ No

Has your financial planner worked with clients in your situation/background?

❏ Yes

❏ No

This has a myriad of meanings, but this could be everything from "lots of student loans" to "entrepreneurs" to "LGBTQIA+" to "BIPOC" to "Millennials" to "First Gen."

Does your financial planner actively listen and take you seriously?

❏ Yes

❏ No

This is a particular area of concern for many women in heterosexual relationships.

It's still entirely too common for a financial planner to largely engage with the male partner instead of with both parties.

Am I comfortable with my financial planner?

❏ Yes

❏ No

This is an incredibly important factor! All the other boxes might be checked, but it still has to be the right fit for you. You can date around and take informational meetings or consultations with a few folks before settling on the right fit. This should be a person who ultimately is in a long-term relationship with you, and you want to feel comfortable.

Helpful Hint: It should be noted that you usually can't get client referrals because of compliance rules precluding a CFP from giving you a client's information. This is a reason you also won't see client testimonials on an advisor's website.

WHERE TO FIND A FINANCIAL PLANNER

XY Planning Network: Cofounded by Alan Moore, MS, CFP, and Michael E. Kitces, MSFS, MTAX, CFP, CLU, ChFC, RHU, REBC, CASL (yeah, it's a lot of designations), XYPN is an organization of fee-only financial advisors specifically focused on Generation X and Generation Y clients. Advisors are required to be both CFPs and fiduciaries and have a signed copy of the oath available on their profiles. There are no asset minimum requirements (meaning you don't have to already be wealthy) and each advisor offers a monthly retainer service. You can also reach your advisor virtually. You can learn more at XYPlanningNetwork.com.

Garrett Planning Network: Founded by Sheryl Garrett, CFP, AIF°, Garrett offers clients access to a network of fee-only, fiduciary CFP professionals. Members of the network do not accept commissions or any other compensation directly from clients. Clients can hire advisors by the hour, which means you can have one-off meetings to address a specific issue if you'd like. There are no income or net worth minimums in order to be a client. You can learn more at GarrettPlanningNetwork.com.

National Association of Personal Financial Advisors (NAPFA): NAPFA was founded in 1983 by a group of advisors interested in creating an organization of highly trained financial professionals who only accepted fee-only compensation. NAPFA is still fee-only financial planners who are also CFPs and fiduciaries. However, you may find that NAPFA advisors do have asset minimums for clients, as there's no particular rule by the organization dictating otherwise. You can learn more at NAPFA.org.

CFP Board's Let's Make a Plan: The CFP Board offers its own tool in order to search CFPs nationwide. You're able to filter based on your location, the type of planning service you need, or the name of a CFP you already know. Let's Make a Plan also offers information to further your education on hiring a financial planner, including overviews of what the planning process looks like and what you should bring with you to your first meeting. You can learn more at letsmakeaplan.org.

I'M NOT READY FOR A FINANCIAL PLANNER

It's okay if you've gone through this chapter and realized you're still not quite ready to hire a financial planner for a long-term relationship. You can use this workbook, the Broke Millennial series, and other personal finance books, podcasts, and resources to help you build your own path for now.

There are planners who offer onetime financial plans to help get you on the right track. If you still want hands-on help, then you could also look into nonprofit credit counselors like the National Foundation for Credit Counseling. Always do your due diligence and research any organization. There are a lot of scams out there and you want to be careful.

Get Your Financial Life Together Check-In

What is your biggest takeaway (or aha moment) from this chapter?

_____.

_____.

_____.

What feels the most overwhelming about this chapter?

_____.

_____.

_____.

Why does it feel so overwhelming to you in this moment?

_____.

_____.

_____.

Based on what you just learned, write down one actionable step you can take this week to improve your financial life.

_____.

_____.

_____.

Epilogue

THIS IS IT. One last moment for me to impart some profound wisdom about how to get your financial life together. Here's the thing: I don't have to. You've put in the work to start building the financial life you want.

Learning how to get your financial life together keeps you from feeling helpless in many situations: being stuck in a job you're ready to leave, staying trapped in the paycheck-to-paycheck cycle, remaining in a bad relationship because you're unable to support yourself, and even passing on poor financial behaviors to the next generation. And the good news is, you're already on the path to getting your financial life together! You've taken the time and energy to educate yourself, face your financial reality, and make a plan to achieve your goals.

I want you to redo an exercise from early in this workbook.

Take a moment to think about money. I know, that sounds a little strange, but just think "money." How does just that word make you feel? Go on, write down a few words to describe how you're feeling right now.

_____.

_____.

_____.

Now take a moment to flip back to page 5 in chapter 2. How did you describe how money made you feel when I first asked?

_____.

_____.

_____.

Hopefully, your feelings—at least one or two—have changed over the course of completing this workbook. It's not a cure-all, but you should be seeing progress. It's okay if money still causes you some anxiety. To be honest, it may always cause you some level of anxiety. But you now have both financial knowledge and the tools to put systems in place to feel in control, which should help you sleep more soundly at night.

Once more, return to pages 16–17 in chapter 2 and reread the goals you set for yourself. Are these goals still the right fit after all the work you've put in? Have you already accomplished some?

Take a moment to either write them down again here *or* set new goals.

In the next 30 days, I will:

_____.

_____.

_____.

In the next six months, I will:

_____.

_____.

_____.

In the next year, I will:

_____.

_____.

_____.

Now cut this section out and tape it up someplace where you'll routinely see it to hold yourself personally accountable.

There will be moments when you stumble or even fall along the way. That's not only okay, but entirely normal. Your financial journey will not be flawless. The key is to assess what went wrong, make a change, and keep pushing forward. The style of this workbook makes it easy to flip back through the previous chapters and exercises when you find yourself in a financial rut or just need a refresher on how to handle a specific money matter.

You can also find more support by reading the rest of the Broke Millennial series including *Broke Millennial, Broke Millennial Takes On Investing,* and *Broke Millennial Talks Money.*

Best of luck on your financial journey!

Erin

Answer Keys

CHAPTER 6: CREDIT MYTH BUSTER

1. Checking my credit report will hurt my score.

   Answer: FALSE.

   No, checking your own credit report(s) will not harm your credit score. It's a smart move for you to be proactive and check your own credit reports from each of the three credit bureaus at least once a year, as allowed by law. You can do this by going to AnnualCreditReport.com.

2. A potential employer can check my credit score.

   Answer: FALSE.

   Your potential employer can run your credit report, and only with your permission. The employer will not be gaining access to your credit score and will receive a truncated version of your actual report.

3. I should carry a balance month to month on my credit card.

   Answer: FALSE.

   Remember: You absolutely, 100 percent, unequivocally do not need to carry over a balance on your credit card to build and maintain a strong credit score. Pay off that card on time and in full every month.

4. It's good to max out my card or get close to the limit.

Answer: FALSE.

Similar to the perversion of carrying a balance, some credit card users believe it shows more responsibility to use as much of the credit limit as possible and then pay it all off. That's like saying it's a good idea to see how many Thai chilies you can stuff in your mouth. (One's enough, trust me.) Keep your utilization at 30 percent of your total available credit limit or less. Preferably less.

5. It's better to just use a prepaid card or a debit card instead of a credit card.

Answer: FALSE.

Prepaid cards and debit cards are not reported to the credit bureaus; therefore, they do not help you establish and build a credit history. So sure, you can use prepaid cards or a debit card as long as you will never need access to credit, which for most people is unrealistic. You can use a mix of credit and debit cards, but I also caution you to be careful about where you swipe your debit card and which ATMs you use. Debit cards leave you far more vulnerable to thieves because they enable people using skimmers (devices used to steal your card information) to gain direct access to your bank account.

6. Don't accept a credit limit increase from your credit card company.

Answer: (probably) FALSE

This depends completely on your ability to handle credit. A credit card company offers you a credit limit increase as a way to lure you into spending more with the hope that you'll ultimately spend more than you can pay off in a month and therefore carry a balance. If you tend to overspend, don't take the risk of the increased credit limit. But if you always make your payments on time and in full, accepting the increase is fine. In fact, it's a simple way to lower your utilization ratio, as long as your spending rate stays the same.

7. Never close your oldest credit card.

Answer: (probably) TRUE

You may outgrow that first credit card—but closing it could cause you to lose the positive history and therefore impact your credit score. If the card has no annual fee, then you might as well keep it open and make an occasional charge to have it stay active. (Yes, banks can close inactive cards and accounts.) If you want to close it, then it's best to have another credit card that you're using properly to keep pumping positive information onto your credit report.

CHAPTER 14: MATCH THE TERMS

GENERAL INVESTING TERMS

1. Compound interest	h
2. Diversification	l
3. Time Horizon	a
4. Risk Tolerance	g
5. Asset Class	n
6. Asset Allocation	i
7. Brokerage	k
8. Equities/stocks/shares	b
9. Sectors	f
10. Bonds	o
11. Index	p
12. Mutual Fund	j
13. Index Fund	m
14. ETF	c
15. Expense Ratio	d
16. Dividend	e

RETIREMENT INVESTING TERMS

1. 401(k)/403(b)/IRA	e
2. Roth	g
3. Traditional	b
4. Employer match	d
5. Vesting schedule	a
6. Immediate	c
7. Cliff	i
8. Graded	j
9. Target date fund	f
10. Early withdrawal penalty	h

Notes

Chapter 2. Is Money a Tinder Date or Marriage Material?

1. The link between your relationship to time and your financial health was studied by MagnifyMoney
   .com and Dr. Philip Zimbardo in 2014.

Chapter 3. Do You Have a Gold Star in Personal Finance?

1. Table taken from Dalton, Michael A., James F. Dalton, Joseph M. Gillice, Thomas P. Langdon, *Fundaments of Financial Planning*, 4th ed. St. Rose, LA: Money Education, 2015, 94.

Chapter 13. How to Negotiate Salary (or Anything Else) by Learning to Ask for What You Want

1. National Labor Relations Board, "National Labor Relations Act . NLRB.gov/how-we-work/national
   -labor-relations-act.

About the Author

DAVID RODGERS

Erin Lowry is the author of *Broke Millennial: Stop Scraping By and Get Your Financial Life Together*; *Broke Millennial Takes On Investing: A Beginner's Guide to Leveling Up Your Money*; and *Broke Millennial Talks Money: Scripts, Stories, and Advice to Navigate Awkward Financial Conversations*. Her first book was named by MarketWatch as one of the best money books of 2017 and by Business Insider as one of the best personal finance books for 2020. She's appeared on CBS *Sunday Morning*, CNBC, and the *Rachael Ray Show*, and has written for *Bloomberg Opinion*, *The New York Times*, *Cosmopolitan*, and *USA Today*. Erin lives in New York City with her husband and their rambunctious dog.

Also by Erin Lowry

"Spot-on, often funny financial advice....
This is the wisdom I wish I had in my twenties and early thirties!"
—LYNNETTE KHALFANI-COX, *New York Times* bestselling author of *Zero Debt*

BROKE
Millennial

STOP SCRAPING BY AND GET
YOUR FINANCIAL LIFE TOGETHER

ERIN LOWRY

BROKE
Millennial
Takes On Investing

A BEGINNER'S GUIDE TO
LEVELING UP YOUR MONEY

ERIN LOWRY

BROKE
Millennial
Talks Money

SCRIPTS, STORIES, AND
ADVICE TO NAVIGATE AWKWARD
FINANCIAL CONVERSATIONS

ERIN LOWRY